OPERATION RESCUE

"Rescue those who are unjustly sentenced to death; don't stand back and let them die"

Proverbs 24:11, TLB

Randall A. Terry

Operation Rescue

Randall A. Terry
Operation Rescue
P.O. Box 1180
Binghamton, New York 13902

Copyright © 1988 by Randall A. Terry
Printed in the United States of America
ISBN: 0-88368-209-5

Photographs supplied by: Lyn Cryderman, Jeanne Robinson, and Operation Rescue. "Human Garbage" and "Suction Abortion at Ten Weeks" used with permission, *Life or Death*, Hayes Publishing Co., Cincinnati, Ohio.

Unless otherwise noted, Scripture quotations are taken from the *New American Standard Bible,* copyright © 1960, 1962, 1963, 1968, 1971, 1972, 1975, 1977, The Lockman Foundation, and are used by permission. Scripture quotations marked *NIV* taken from the *New International Version* copyright © 1973, 1978, 1984, International Bible Society are used by permission. Scripture quotations marked *TLB* are taken from *The Living Bible,* copyright © 1971 by Tyndale House Publishers, Wheaton, Illinois, and are used by permission. Cover verse marked *TLB* is taken from *The Living Bible* copyright © 1971 owned by assignment by Illinois Marine Bank N.A. (as trustee). Used by permission of Tyndale House Publishers, Inc., Wheaton, IL 60189.

The views of the author are not necessarily the views of Whitaker House.

Dedication

To the "Baby Does" arrested and jailed in Atlanta for trying to prevent murder during the summer of 1988. Your courage and dedication may prove to be the turning point in this war against child killing.

And also, more importantly, to the babies—some dead, some alive, some yet to be conceived—that these dear rescuers are standing for. It is the cry of my innermost being that multitudes of children will be born and not killed as a result of Operation Rescue.

"Let this be written for a future generation, that a people not yet created may praise the Lord" (Psalm 102:18, NIV).

Acknowledgments

I want to acknowledge the tremendous sacrifice my wife has made for me to engage in this battle. I love her and thank God for her.

I also want to recognize the hard work and loyal friendship of Gary, Mary, Debbie, Barbara, Marti, Mark, Barbara, Joe, Lynn, Dan, Judy, their spouses, and so many others for making the vision of Operation Rescue a reality. History will be different because of the children saved through their labor and prayers.

In addition, let us all acknowledge those brave souls who have been rescuing for over ten years—especially Joan Andrews—in an hour when rescues were not "acceptable." Their courage is a beacon and example to us all.

Foreword

by Pat Robertson

We live in a time when Christian values are being ridiculed and where life is being cheapened. The great philosopher Francis Schaeffer, before his death, urged that it was time for Christians to become involved more than ever before in the course of affairs in our nation.

Randy Terry has begun the same dramatic nonviolent protest against the slaughter of innocent babies in our nation that brought racial justice and equality in the 1960s.

I commend him for his boldness and applaud the goal of Operation Rescue to save the lives of one and a half million unborn children who are slaughtered in our land every year.

Pat Robertson
Founder, Chairman, and Chief Executive Officer
The Christian Broadcasting Network, Inc.

Foreword

by Dr. D. James Kennedy

Abortion has become *the* issue in this country, for if you lose life, you lose all. If Christians do not win on this issue, we will not win on any issue.

The shocking reality is that Christians could stop abortions today if they wanted to.

If four million Christians went tomorrow and stood as a visible presence in front of every abortion clinic in the land, no babies would be killed. Even if everyone were arrested for this courageous stand for God's truth, our already overcrowded jails would not be able to hold this number.

Thankfully, in many cities Christians are putting feet to their faith and are doing just this in obedience to Proverbs 24:11 that tells us to rescue the innocent who are being dragged to the slaughter. These courageous individuals have become known as Operation Rescue.

They place their bodies between the abortionist and his victims, rescuing the innocent babies from their impending dismemberment. They are modeling Christ's example of placing His body between the sinner and the gates of hell. They are living out the parable of the Good Samaritan who got physically involved in the suffering of a stranger.

Operation Rescue is an organization of volunteers all across America who have said, ''Enough is enough.'' They peacefully surround abortion chambers in large numbers, praying and singing, making it impossible for the abortionists to enter the building to kill children. When the police come to arrest them, the protesters go limp, making it necessary for the officers to carry them away. This often takes several hours.

I feel this approach is biblically correct. These peaceful protesters are obeying God's law in a peaceful, nonviolent manner. As a result no babies are killed at the abortion clinic while the protesters are there. In addition, the pro-life movement gains momentum, adding to the social pressure necessary to bring about political change.

I consider Operation Rescue a legitimate front-line force in the pro-life movement. Please prayerfully consider joining with me in supporting this organization to save the lives of the unborn and to stop the killing permanently.

Let us not repeat the lesson of the German church in the 1930s and 40s that stood apathetically by and watched as the unwanted of their generation were marched off to unspeakable death. We need Corrie Ten Booms of the 1980s who will stand up to man's repudiation of God's law and follow Jesus' command to love our neighbors as ourselves.

May God give us the courage and grace to take a stand during these last critical days of America—for the sake of the unborn, for our children, for ourselves, and for Jesus Christ.

Dr. D. James Kennedy
Senior Minister
Coral Ridge Presbyterian Church
Fort Lauderdale, Florida

Foreword
by Jerry Falwell

I believe that non-violent civil disobedience is the wave of the future for the pro-life movement in this country. Operation Rescue may be God's way of combatting this national sin of abortion. I have come to know Randall Terry and many other godly men and women who are giving of themselves unselfishly on behalf of this defenseless minority—the innocent unborn.

After fifteen years of various efforts to judicially and legislatively reverse *Roe vs. Wade,* Operation Rescue is a breath of fresh air. At first, their efforts were not taken very seriously, but their courage and convictions have brought national attention to this critical issue.

Operation Rescue is, and always will be, controversial. But I believe they are right because man's laws permitting abortion are in clear violation of God's higher laws.

I urge you to carefully read this book and prayerfully consider what role you might play in this effort to stop the abortion holocaust.

Jerry Falwell
Pastor, Thomas Road Baptist Church
Founder, Moral Majority
Chancellor, Liberty University

Contents

Appendixes

Preface

I wrote this book from jail.

Not jail in Russia, or in Communist China, but in America—in Binghamton, New York.

Why was I arrested? Because I dared to set foot inside an abortion clinic and offer pregnant mothers an alternative before they had their children killed. I was charged with criminal trespass, tried, and found guilty.

In 1978 when I entered Bible school to prepare for the ministry, who would have imagined that God's call on my life would take me behind bars—not as a visitor but as an inmate?

I had not intended to get involved in pro-life ministry, but the Lord often refocuses our calling in life as we seek His will.

After graduating from Elim Bible Institute in 1981, I married my wife Cindy and we were planning to be missionaries. I had previously traveled to Central America twice, and we had a standing invitation to join an established work in Mexico.

In the fall of 1983, God interrupted our plans to be missionaries and called us to the mission field of abortion clinics. He called us to reach out to the women facing crisis pregnancies and to save the lives of the precious children who were scheduled to meet an untimely death at the hands of the abortionists.

This book is about God's command to His people to love their neighbor as themselves. This book is about murder and how we can rescue the innocent from death. This book is also about the conflict between man's laws and God's laws and what the Bible says we should do.

Before you make any hasty judgments about whether I'm right or wrong, please read this book. Try to grasp the purpose, spirit, and intent of rescue missions, and then ask yourself, "What would God have me do?"

1
Small Beginnings

How Operation Rescue Began

1

Small Beginnings

How Operation Rescue Began

When my wife and I began Project Life in May 1984, our vision was threefold:

> First, to do everything possible to rescue babies and their mothers from the nightmare of abortion on the very doorstep of local abortion clinics.
>
> Second, to show the love of Christ to women in crisis pregnancies by providing whatever help they need to carry their child to term.
>
> Third, to re-educate the public and the church to the value of human life from a Bible-based, Christian perspective and to expose the horrors of abortion.

I began standing outside abortion clinics on my lunch hours and days off, trying to persuade women to choose life for their children. At the beginning of June my wife joined me. For the next four months she stood outside the clinics over forty hours a week trying to rescue the unborn who were imminently facing death.

For the first several weeks our efforts were completely futile. Finally, one young woman listened to us and decided not to keep her appointment at the clinic that day. Our elation later turned to sorrow when she returned the next week to have her child killed.

After that another young woman pretended to be going in for an abortion. We were able to persuade her, so we thought, and turn her away. Later we discovered that she was planted by the abortion clinic to hear what we were telling their clients.

Then another young woman turned away, and once again to our utter dismay and heartache she, too, went back and had her child killed. It seemed the work God had called us to was going to be filled with constant hopelessness and despair.

Reinforcements to the Rescue

In the beginning weeks, Cindy and I stood alone in front of the abortion mill. As the abortuary personnel began to perceive us as a threat to their business, they rallied some radical pro-abortionists to deter us. When we tried to talk to the pregnant women, these people would harass my wife and me by following us around and jumping between us and the clients.

In the midst of this harassment and discouragement, the brothers and sisters at our home church—The Church at Pierce Creek—rallied around us. We organized a picket-making session and made pro-life signs. Then one morning, to the astonishment of the clinic personnel, we showed up with thirty other people who were picketing, singing, praying, and standing with us.

The extra strength in numbers had a tremendous effect on our adversaries and on the community. The local media covered the event, showing all the protesters in front of the abortion clinic.

We were thrilled by the publicity, but we were not saving lives. Still, our small group continued picketing the local abortion mill, praying fervently, and trying to rescue children from death and their mothers from exploitation.

Finally, toward the end of that summer, the seemingly impenetrable wall began to crack. In a two-week period five young women who were pregnant and planning to abort their children turned away and chose life for their babies. We were ecstatic! Those five children and mothers were the first among hundreds who would be rescued in the years to come.

A New Vision

In October 1984, we opened The Crisis Pregnancy Center six days a week to offer women free pregnancy tests, confidential counseling, baby clothes, baby furniture, baby formula, and a wide spectrum of referrals so that a woman who wanted to keep her baby could do so with support from others.

More importantly, we felt it was critical to reach the expectant mothers with the facts before the abortion propagandists deceived them with their lies and half-truths. By offering free pregnancy tests we were able to talk with many young women who were still undecided about what to do with their children. After hearing the truth from one of our counselors, most made solid decisions for life.

Then the Lord placed in our hearts a new vision—a home for unwed mothers where we could house those who had no place to go if they wanted to keep their children. At first pregnant girls were placed with families in private homes. It wasn't until later, in the fall of 1987, that The House of Life became a reality.

As a result of our outreach, we were involved in extensive pro-life work—speaking to concerned groups, showing films, preaching, appearing on television, talking on radio shows, being interviewed by the newspaper, educating people on abortion, instructing people how to lobby—doing all the things that an active, involved pro-life ministry should do.

The First Rescue Mission

In the midst of all this activity, the Lord started to speak to us about His law being higher than man's law. We began to wrestle with our responsibility to obey God's Word above and beyond our obedience to man's laws. At that time we started discussing a possible rescue mission.

A rescue mission happens when one or two, or a group of twenty or a hundred or a thousand people go to an abortion clinic to prevent the slaughter of innocent lives.

In January 1986, seven of us participated in our first rescue mission. We arrived at the abortion clinic just after it opened and before any patients came. Then we locked ourselves in one of the inner rooms.

Before long, the police arrived and asked us to leave. When we declined, they carried us out. Everyone was charged with criminal trespass and resisting arrest because we went limp and would not walk out of the building. Our convictions did not allow us to assist the police in our removal from a place where children would die. Had we walked out, the abortion clinic would have immediately started its bloody work.

At the time, we felt this was the best approach to take. Entering an abortion mill, however, increases the risk that false accusations may be made and additional charges brought against rescuers. So caution is advised.

Jolting the Community

Our first rescue mission jolted the Christian community. Until then we had been held in high regard and honor because of our efforts and sacrifice on behalf of the unborn. They felt we had "broken the law." (We'll discuss later why we maintain that we are not breaking the law.) Our actions left a lot of pastors and congregations in a state of shock and confusion. Others were downright angry.

I can't blame them. Long hours of searching the Scriptures, praying, and studying history preceded my understanding of the validity of rescue missions. Gradually, I saw that when man's laws and God's law conflict, the believer has a responsibility and an obligation to obey God rather than man.

Before we had our first rescue mission, I spent considerable time discussing my thoughts with my pastor, Rev. Daniel J. Little. All of our activities met with his blessing. In fact, three weeks after our first rescue mission, we staged a second one in which Pastor Little and his wife Judy participated along with several other people. This caused an even greater stir in the community because a respected clergyman and not just a "small band of radicals" had been arrested for the cause of life.

Only God knows how much it has meant to my wife and me to be associated with a pastor and a church who have stood with us through thick and thin. I've told many people over the years that the reason we've not gone astray or become disheartened is because of The Church at Pierce Creek. The prayers and fellowship of the saints have sustained us through the heartache and the challenges of prolife ministry.

Losing on Every Front

While awaiting trial, our involvement with pro-life work continued. By then our ministry included operating The Crisis Pregnancy Center, picketing, sidewalk counseling, educating people, producing literature, and even doing an occasional rescue mission.

During the spring of 1986, I realized that, in spite of our efforts and those of thousands across the country, we were losing the war. In fact, we were losing on almost every front.

We were losing more babies. As a result of *Roe vs. Wade* and subsequent court decisions, a baby could now be legally aborted up until the day of birth. Infanticide is practiced in most hospitals with more than four thousand children murdered every day.

We were losing more teenagers. School-based clinics could now dispense contraceptives to minors and refer pregnant teens for abortions without their parents' notification or consent. While schools cannot dispense an aspirin to a student without written permission, they can make an appointment for a young girl to have her child killed—a major medical procedure that could leave permanent physical and emotional scars—and her parents would never know.

We were losing our conscience as a nation. Abortionists have now entered into the ghoulish practice of harvesting organs from aborted babies—babies who are often still alive! After these tiny infants somehow survive vaginal or Caesarean Section abortions, their organs are removed (without any anesthesia to numb the pain) and sold for a profit to research organizations or hospitals.

This devaluing of human life in America is laying the groundwork for another horrible practice—euthanasia. An alarming number of elderly and disabled people are already being starved to death—a painful and agonizing way to die. Unless Christians speak out and take action, the next stage could be lethal injection for those unwanted by society.

With these facts in mind, I began to ask the Lord some questions: What must we in the pro-life movement do in order to win? What would it take to obtain a constitutional amendment to outlaw child killing in this country once again?

The answer to my prayers and questions came over a period of several months.

I remember sharing with my pastor and his wife that God was placing a vision in my heart whereby we might once again secure justice for the children and dignity for the mothers. This vision didn't crystalize all at once but slowly came into focus, much like the blind man in Mark 8:24 who first saw "men like trees walking" before his sight was totally restored.

Doing Time

The seven of us who were arrested at the first rescue were tried and found guilty. Everyone agreed to pay the sixty dollar fine except me. I refused and was sent to jail.

Sometimes I felt good about being in jail, in the sense that the apostles said that they rejoiced to be found worthy to suffer shame for His name. It encouraged me to think about other great Christians who had been imprisoned because they obeyed God and stood up for what was right.

At other times I experienced feelings of intense anger and frustration. Forced to stay behind bars with criminals all around me, I felt a terrible sense of injustice. I was in jail for trying to save babies from death and mothers from exploitation, while the killers (wrongly called doctors) were on the outside free!

In jail there is no such thing as privacy or peace and quiet. The cell block area was constantly filled with cigarette smoke and rock music. But in the midst of this harsh, crowded environment were some very lonely men with desperate needs. While I was in jail, I did my best to be a consistent witness for Jesus Christ, and God gave me several opportunities to share the gospel with inmates whose hearts were open. I also had plenty of time to read, study, and write.

In the spring, I spent ten days in jail. Later during July and August, I was interned for twenty-two days as a result of another rescue mission. Then, just before my daughter was born, a lawyer got me released on appeal, which we eventually lost. I served the remaining twenty-three days of my sentence in March and April of 1987.

What We Needed

By the end of my jail term in the summer of 1986, I had a more definite idea of what it was going to take to secure justice again for the children.

First of all, I felt we needed a repentance in the church that would result in a national uprising against abortion. As Christians, I knew we needed to beg God's forgiveness for allowing this holocaust to continue unchallenged for fifteen years. We had allowed man's laws to dictate that we would turn our backs on those who were being killed instead of loving our neighbors as ourselves.

We as Christians had to repent because we were so concerned about our image and our appearance before the community that we were not willing to stop an atrocity, an injustice, a holocaust of such major proportions that it's now five times greater than the Nazi slaughter of the Jews.

Secondly, I saw that if we believed abortion was murder, then we needed to act like it was murder. The logical response when you or I see someone being killed is to do what we can to physically intervene and save them.

I also realized that the pro-life movement was not creating the tension and upheaval necessary to produce political and social change. We were being too nice. Our actions and our rhetoric were so far removed from one another that we did not deserve a fair hearing.

Once we repented and started rescuing, I knew that besides saving babies and mothers, our actions would have the secondary benefit of creating positive social tension.

Pro-lifers were saying that abortion was murder, and yet all we were doing about it was writing a letter now and then. If my little girl was about to be murdered, I certainly would not write a letter to the editor! I would dive in with both hands and feet and do whatever was necessary to save her life.

We were all clamoring about abortion being murder, but we had not even peacefully tried to blockade abortion mills. As these ideas took shape in my mind and the truths of God's Word grabbed my heart, the foundation for Operation Rescue was laid.

Mixed Reviews

In November of 1986, I told a few friends and fellow pro-life workers the vision God had placed in my heart for Operation Rescue. My burden included reaching the pastoral community and local churches with the call to repent, and then giving them a practical way to put their repentance into action—by peacefully staging sit-ins at abortion mills.

The vision met with mixed reviews. Some people thought it was great. Others thought large rescues could never be pulled off. "We don't have enough pastoral involvement, and we don't have the numbers," some lamented.

At that point the number of people involved in rescues had been ten here, twenty there. The largest rescue mission up to that time had been 106 people in St. Louis in 1986.

A lot of people said we were crazy. Others latched onto the idea and saw Operation Rescue as a catalyst that would end the abortion holocaust. We produced some literature, spread the vision, and started calling on people to join us.

In the spring of 1987, I shared my vision with a brother in Christian leadership. He challenged me to test our tactics on a smaller scale before we did our first major series of rescues in New York City in May of 1988. I took his advice, and we decided to do something in the fall of 1987 that would help spark momentum and demonstrate that rescue missions could work.

Target: Cherry Hill

We set our sights on the Philadelphia area for the Thanksgiving weekend of 1987 and began to recruit. Our efforts paid off!

On November 28, nearly three hundred people blocked the Cherry Hill Women's Clinic in Cherry Hill, New Jersey—just over the river outside of Philadelphia.

All the pro-abortion forces knew we were coming into the Philadelphia area. As a result, two abortion clinics shut down for fear we would arrive there; another one had sixty police posted outside. But Cherry Hill Women's Center was sitting vulnerable and unprotected when we arrived at six o'clock in the morning.

Before long, nearly three hundred rescuers had sealed off access to the building. We sang, prayed, read psalms, and basically had a church service on the doorstep of hell for nearly eleven hours! No babies died. It was glorious, peaceful, and prayerful.

When the police arrived, they were as bewildered as they were overwhelmed. They did not have the manpower to deal with us. From six o'clock to ten thirty, they let us sing and pray without making any arrests. Eventually we were told the abortion clinic was threatening the police with a lawsuit if they didn't arrest us.

At ten thirty, the police began carrying people away one at a time. Mothers, fathers, grandmothers, grandfathers, and singles were arrested for saving babies from death. All were charged with trespassing and later released.

Our group left Cherry Hill charged up, full of vision, and bubbling over with excitement. We had successfully closed down an abortion center for an entire day. No children were killed there that day. No women were exploited.

The sidewalk counselors told me three mothers changed their minds and ultimately chose life for their babies because we were there. Lives were saved because people willfully placed their bodies between the victims and the murderers.

The Turning Point

Cherry Hill marked a turning point in the Christian community's response to Operation Rescue. The results were significant in several areas.

1. Because the demonstrations were peaceful, prayerful, and involved the clergy, the Christian community began to take a more positive view of rescue missions.
2. The Christian media's response was overwhelming. Several periodicals, such as *People of Destiny; Maranatha; The National Catholic Register;* and *Christianity Today* ran articles on the Cherry Hill effort. CBN's *The 700 Club* did a feature story on Operation Rescue.
3. Passive pro-lifers who were discouraged and inactive caught the vision and saw that they could actually put an end to the senseless killing of children and the exploitation of mothers.
4. People who had never before been involved in pro-life work but had always thought abortion was wrong were finally getting involved. Many came straight from the pew to sitting in front of the abortuary door saying to God, "Please forgive me for my apathy;" and to the abortionist, "As long as I'm here, you're not going to kill innocent children."

Now that we were off and running, recruitment for the New York City rescue scheduled for May of 1988 became easier. Excitement grew, and so did the number of clergymen who were willing to participate. In the end, over twenty protestant pastors, fifteen Roman Catholic priests, two monsignors, an auxillary bishop, four nuns, an Orthodox priest, and two rabbis decided to rescue children with us and allow themselves to be arrested.

Noise from the Enemy Camp

As we set our sights toward New York, the media and the Christian community weren't the only ones interested in our activity. The entire abortion industry along with the National Organization for Women began to sit up and take notice.

The closer we got to the rescue date, the more vicious our opponents became. The abortionists threatened us with bodily harm and tried to intimidate us by seeking injunctions to block our peaceful demonstrations. The so-called "pro-choice" groups launched an all-out campaign to stop the rescue.

The opponents of Operation Rescue take our stand seriously. Why? Because they know if we can call enough people to repent and participate in a mass uprising to shut down abortion mills, their government funding will be cut off and their selfish "pro-choice" murders will once again be made illegal.

It's been said that a man can judge his true worth by his enemies. Our enemies are determined, organized, and vicious. They are well-supported by politicians and highly financed by the abortion industry (a $700 million a year business). They are also scared and angry. But if God is for us, who can be against us?

Counting the Cost

One phrase from our Declaration of Independence has become very real to me: "We pledge our lives, our fortunes, and our sacred honors." If we are going to end this war against children, we must be willing to surrender our lives, our selfish ways, our finances, and our reputations.

Will America be spared the full fury of God's wrath over this bloodshed? Will we be chastened and restored? Or will we be destroyed? The answer to a great degree lies with you and me. Our future depends on our willingness to make the sacrifices necessary to make the rescue movement successful.

God's people must rise up with one heart, one voice, as one body, and say, "Enough is enough. Oh, Lord, we have sinned. We've allowed this holocaust to go on. Please forgive us." I believe our repentance will move the heart of God in such a way that He will show mercy in the midst of judgment.

From the platform of repentance, we must take our bodies down to the abortion mills and peacefully and prayerfully place ourselves between the killer and his intended victims. This is the only way we can produce the social tension necessary to bring about political change.

God help us in this critical hour.

2
We're Being Watched

Jeanne Robinson

Putting Our Generation Into Perspective

2

We're Being Watched

Putting Our Generation into Perspective

We're being watched. Everything we do is being recorded. By the CIA? By the FBI? No. By the courts of heaven.

I call this "The Chronicles of the Kingdom of Heaven." Every one of us can be found on those pages, and some day our motives, actions, thoughts, and whole lives (excluding sins repented of) will be exposed at the judgment seat of Christ.

We're also being watched by those around us. The press and people in business, politics, and education are scrutinizing the church. Fellow believers, Christian media, and most importantly, our children are watching us. Both the converted and unconverted are making judgments concerning Christians in America.

In addition, the next generation will weigh our lives against our words, our deeds against our doctrines, our strength and courage against this hour of crisis.

When that occurs, what will the next generation think? What will be their gut level reaction toward us? How will future generations remember those of us living today?

How will tomorrow's children view the current social and political leaders? In what light will future Christians see contemporary leaders of the church or today's average evangelical for that matter?

Looking Back in Disgrace

Tomorrow's opinions and judgments about those of us living today may be startlingly different from our own. We need to look back only one generation to support the different perspective that time gives us. For example, how do we view the German Christians who stood by and did nothing to rescue Jews from mass slaughter?

Let's make it personal. How do *you* feel about church-going Christians who turned out Jewish believers because they feared being investigated or persecuted by the Nazis?

Trainloads of Jews often passed churches on their way to the death camps. What is *your* opinion of Christians who only sang louder to drown out the Jews' desperate cries for help? What do *you* think of the following statement issued by the German Lutheran bishops?

> "We German Protestant Christians accept the saving of our nation by our leader Adolf Hitler as a gift from God's hand." They affirmed "unanimously our unlimited fealty [loyalty] to the Third Reich and its leader."[1]

The praise and accommodation given Hitler by much of the clergy and church in Germany now stands as a disgrace to the Church of Jesus Christ. Yet *in that hour*, extolling Hitler, compromising with him, and ignoring the plight of the Jews was the *acceptable norm* for most Christians and church leaders.

What the Church Tolerates

Herein lies a fearful truth: *What the church tolerates today, she may be despised for tomorrow.* The "acceptable norm'' for a weak and compromising church becomes the blight of future generations.

With embarrassment modern Christians remember the eighteenth century clergy and congregations who owned slaves. The light of history shamefully exposes the fearful Dutch Reformed minister who refused to help Corrie Ten Boom hide a young Jewish mother and her baby because it was dangerous and ''illegal.''

Throughout Europe a compromising clergy lulled their congregations to sleep, convincing them by argument, by silence, and by example that confrontation with Nazi Germany and their godless laws should be avoided at all costs. Injustice, violence, and oppression should have a deaf ear and a blind eye turned to them.

These ministers fed their flocks spiritual chaff, persuading them not to face reality. Pastors who preferred convenience to conviction offered a Christ who was passive and weak; a Jesus who ignored the orphan, the widow, and the oppressed; a Messiah who was mainly concerned with the temporal and eternal happiness of His people.

Bonhoeffer: Hero or Traitor?

In stark contrast history remembers the courage and faithfulness of Dietrich Bonhoeffer, a young German pastor who lived during the rise and fall of the Third Reich. He warned his contemporaries, rebuked fellow ministers for compromise, and helped start a ''free synod'' of German churches who dissented against Hitler and government policies.

Bonhoeffer ran an illegal pastoral training school in his home after such schools were forbidden by law. He smuggled Jews to safety and freedom, and finally was martyred for his work against Hitler about one week before the war ended.

Throughout those dreadful years, Bonhoeffer was not looked on with favor by most of his contemporary ministers. He was a constant irritation to their safe, smooth Christianity, and their compromise with sin and Satan. The government watched him closely and eventually executed him as a traitor. Now he towers as a hero over his contemporaries.

Whose Opinion Counts?

We must remember that the light of history conveys not only facts, but an "editorial" feeling about someone's life, especially during a time of crisis. Some people may have been helped and even converted through the ministries of clergy or congregations who compromised during slavery or the holocaust.

Perhaps some of those churches had wonderful covered dish dinners or stirring seminars on eschatology. But now, from a distance, the light of history casts a hue of contempt over their lives and ministries. Why? Because in a season of crisis, they failed to stand for the whole counsel of God, and they fled when faced with adversity.

The fact is, the amount of praise or contempt a man receives from his contemporaries is not an accurate gauge of how he will be remembered. Tomorrow's opinions and judgments about those of us living today may be startlingly different from our own. In fact, history often ignores the sentiments of contemporaries. Many men we now despise as villains were praised by their contemporaries, while those we now herald as heroes often suffered vicious persecution and hatred from those living in the same hour.

Who can forget the scenes of thousands of youth chanting their praise to Hitler? Many of Hitler's contemporaries in Germany adored him. Josef Goebbels wrote of Hitler in his diary:

> He is a genius. The natural creative instrument of
> a fate determined by God. I am deeply moved: He

is like a child, kind, good, merciful. Like a cat: cunning, clever, agile. Like a lion: roaring and great and gigantic. A fellow, a man![2]

Ironically, even church history is filled with men and women of conviction who suffered persecution from fellow believers for cutting against the grain of nominal Christianity. Spurgeon, Whitefield, and Wesley, once scorned by their contemporaries both inside and outside the church, are now regarded as heroes of the faith.

This brings us to a very searching question: When the praise or disdain of our contemporaries is spent, and our lives are over, how will we be viewed in the light of history? How will Christians thirty, forty, or one hundred years from now view the average churchgoer, pastor, or television preacher who lived during the 1960s, 1970s, and 1980s? What legacy of courage will our local churches leave behind? What heritage of spirit will we leave our children and our grandchildren?

Understanding the Times

Most believers would agree that America lies in a very serious, even critical state morally. While our nation sinks in a swamp of immorality and cruelty, most of the church continues with business as usual—Bible studies, prayer meetings, covered dish dinners, and Holy Land tours. These activities aren't bad, but when we ignore the crucial issues of our day, we become shallow and irrelevant.

God isn't interested in the amount of "good" activity we generate in a crisis, no matter how much it seems to be blessed.

Noah's generation faced a moral watershed in which "the Lord saw that the wickedness of man was great upon the earth, and that every intent of the thoughts of his heart was only evil continually" (Genesis 6:5). Yet Jesus observed that "they were eating and drinking, they were marrying and giving in marriage until the day that Noah entered the ark, and *they did not understand* until the flood came and took them all away" (Matthew 24:38,39, italics added).

We cannot afford to be uninformed and complacent until judgment strikes. The church needs to be like the "men of Issachar, who *understood* the times and knew what Israel should do" (1 Chronicles 12:32).

God always calls His people to *action* in times of moral crisis. He is not pleased by our good intentions, as noble as they may seem; He is pleased by our obedience.

What Are We Doing?

So what is the average Christian *doing* to stem the tide of moral insanity? Have you written to your congressman, voted intelligently, examined your child's school curriculum, picketed an adult bookstore, or fought for the rights of the unborn?

Are you even informed on these crucial issues? Many Christians, spiritualizing their walk with God, don't feel called to "social issues."

If America continues to disintegrate morally and socially, if human, religious, and parental rights keep being stripped away, future Christians—our children and grandchildren—will look back and say,

> "Dear God, what were the Christians in America thinking? What were they doing? While they rushed to hear the message of peace and prosperity, unborn babies were killed by the millions, handicapped newborns and the elderly were starved to death, and children were being exploited by pornography. How could they have stood by and done so little? Didn't they care? Why didn't they protect the innocent and join in the

battle for truth and righteousness? Why did
they stand by as our freedoms were being stripped
away?''

What is the average pastor *doing* to equip his people to
deal with the critical battles that are raging across our nation?
Most ministers are not preparing the saints to deal with the
issues at hand. In making mention of some of our country's
more glaring sins such as abortion, pornography, or
homosexuality, pastors usually do not give Christians a clear
agenda and example of *action,* but simply denounce these
sins from a theological standpoint.

Most ministers present a passive Christ who is willing to
leave unchallenged the cruelty and wickedness permeating
our society—a Christ who ignores the million and a half
children who are slaughtered each year in the abortion
holocaust. And Christians will gladly follow a Christ who
does not show them practical ways to get involved. Why?
Because practical action is *costly,* calling for confrontation,
persecution, sacrifice, and suffering.

One Life at a Time

At a rescue that we conducted in Binghamton, New York,
twenty brave souls arrived at the abortion clinic by 6:30 a.m.
and used their cars to block the front door and the driveway, making it impossible for the clients to drive in.

In the midst of the commotion of police cars and tow
trucks, a young woman drove up who was scheduled to have
her child killed that morning. The girl was accompanied
by her sister and her sister's two children.

As she approached the driveway, I walked up to her car
and said, ''Hi. A bunch of people parked their cars here so
that no abortions could take place. They really care about
you, and have ways to help you.'' Then I politely asked,
''Would you please go next door to that donut shop? I'd like
to talk to you for a minute.''

She pulled into the parking lot, and another woman and I went over to talk with her. She and her sister got out of the car, holding the two children. For the next half an hour, I pleaded with her. Twice I literally got on my knees and plead for the life of her unborn child.

"Suzie, these twenty people have risked arrest and will go to jail for you and your baby. Please come to our crisis pregnancy center for just half an hour." We continued talking. I kept pleading. She was hard.

Finally, she agreed. "Great!" I exclaimed. "Let's go!" and I jumped in their car. We drove to one of our crisis pregnancy centers, and I left her with one of our counselors. She stayed and viewed the powerful pro-life film, *A Matter of Choice*. At the end of three hours she left *still undecided* about giving life to her baby. This was one tough case.

One week later, our counselor got a call. "Hello, Barb? It's me, Suzie. What was that doctor's name you said would help me? I've decided to keep my baby." Glory to God! The child's life was spared!

If we had not done the rescue mission, that child would be dead. It's that simple. Because twenty brave people chose to obey God rather than men, a human being was saved.

Years from now, who would dare tell that child, "Those people who 'broke the law' were wrong! You should have been killed!"

Dying in the Ditch

Considering the current mindset of the church in staying decidedly uninvolved in "social issues," if the parable of the Good Samaritan were re-written today, it would probably read like this:

A certain man was going down from Queens to the Bronx, and he fell among robbers. They stripped him and beat him and left him half dead. By chance, a certain clergyman was traveling on that road, and when he saw the injured man, he was too busy with the work of the Lord to help him, so he passed by on the other side.

A few steps later, the clergyman encountered a man with a "Right to Street" petition, deploring the fact that men could be beaten up and left to die in the ditch. He gladly signed the petition (this being a sop for his conscience) and went on his way.

As he traveled, he pondered what had become of society that such an unjust and barbaric crime could be committed. When he arrived home, the clergyman dug into his library of books. The more he read and thought, the more he became convinced that the root of this atrocity was humanism, secular humanism.

The clergyman developed a series of sermons showing secular humanism to be the root of all ditch beatings, killings, and other social evils. The messages were rich in the meat of the Scriptures and proved quite inspirational to his congregation.

An elder in his church so thoroughly enjoyed the series that he sent a cassette to Behemoth Bible Publishing House. The editorial staff listened to the stirring message and unanimously agreed that the sermon and the minister were brilliant. They contacted him immediately, offered him a contract, and requested he write a book entitled, *Humanism: The Root of Ditch Beatings.*

The minister, viewing this as the hand of God, completed the book in two months. As everyone expected, it became an overnight bestseller. Requests began pouring in for the minister to give lectures and expose the evils of this humanistic philosophy. He began to crisscross the country, recounting that fateful night of inspiration when he passed the man dying in the ditch. His book, lectures, and charismatic personality thrust him into prominence. He was a hero!

Well, a hero to everyone but the man in the ditch.

Shortly after the clergyman passed by, a gospel singer came upon the beaten man. Since he did not feel that God had called him to "social issues," he said a prayer for the man, passed by on the other side, signed the "Right to Street" petition, and continued on his way.

As he journeyed, the injured man's moans and cries for help haunted his mind. "Should I have stopped?" the singer asked himself. "No," he answered. "God has not called me to a ditch ministry." But the feelings of concern for that man still ate at his conscience. He was so moved that he began writing a song. He got home and hammered out the chords and the melody, and soon sang it in his local church. People cried as they listened. Many testified it was the most moving song they had ever heard. He entitled it "Dying in the Ditch."

Being encouraged by his friends, the gospel singer mailed a demo tape to Salt of the Earth Records. They immediately offered him a contract, and he recorded an album. The title cut, "Dying in the Ditch," soared to the top of the charts, and he toured the country, singing to sympathetic, weeping crowds. He won a Dove and a Grammy award for the best religious song. He became a hero.

Unfortunately, the man in the ditch died.

Some time later, another man was beaten and left to die in the same ditch. A certain layman was driving to church when he noticed him. He felt compassion for him, hit the brakes, and came to his aid. He put peroxide and ointment on his wounds, loaded him into his car, getting blood and mud all over the seats, and took him to the emergency ward of the nearest hospital. He said, "Take care of him. When I come back, I'll pay the bill." He then went to church, elated he had rescued a fellow man from death.

When he arrived at church, the ushers scolded him for having blood and mud on his suit. He gave a brief explanation, with which they were unimpressed, and went to sit down. During the testimony time, he stood to his feet and related his amazing story. Everyone noticed the dirt and blood stains on his suit. He was an embarrassment.

Before he was finished, the pastor interrupted by asking, "Were you able to lead him in a sinner's prayer?" The layman explained that the injured man had been nearly unconscious, but he would try when he went to visit him. He attempted to finish his story, but the pastor interrupted again, saying, "Brother, we will have to hear the rest of your story on another occasion. We want to give our guest speaker plenty of time."

Then, turning to the congregation, the pastor said, "Today's guest speaker has a tremendous command of the Scriptures. He is a famous author and lecturer, a gifted man, a hero in the church. He has come to talk to us today about secular humanism."

That's Not My Calling

We must understand that men and women have different ministries and callings. But in a time of crisis, all are called to sacrifice. Perhaps the priest and Levite of the Good Samaritan parable sought to silence their conscience for not helping the wounded, beaten man by telling themselves, "I'm not called to a ditch ministry. I'm called to preach the Word." But would God accept such an excuse?

Likewise, our society is beaten, bleeding, and dying in the ditch while millions of Christians and their leaders do little or nothing to lift it out, dress its wounds, and work for its restoration.

Martin Luther is credited with saying:

> If I profess with the loudest voice and the clearest exposition every portion of the truth of God except precisely that little point which the world and the devil are at the moment attacking, I am not confessing Christ, however boldly I may be

professing Christ. Where the battle rages, there the
loyalty of the soldier is proved, and to be steady
on all the battlefield besides, is mere flight and
disgrace if he flinches at that point.

How will the courts of heaven remember each of us
individually? What will the Lord Jesus say when He looks
at our lives? How will your children and your grandchildren view your response to this current holocaust? Will they
see your example of courage, sacrifice, and love for your
neighbor? Will you be remembered as one who helped end
abortion and turn America back to God? Or will you be just
another face in a sea of self-centered Christians who stood
by while millions of children were killed and our nation
collapsed into hell?

May it be the former, my friend. Children's lives are at
stake. The survival of America may be at stake. But if we
stand together, time still exists to restore justice and to lead
America out of moral chaos, turning her back to godliness
and common decency.

3
The Salt of the Earth

Jeanne Robinson

What is the Church
Called to Do?

3

The Salt of the Earth

What is the Church Called to Do?

What makes a "spiritual giant"? In your church, besides your pastor, who are the most admired and respected "spiritual pillars" in the congregation? Think about it.

In most of our assemblies, those heralded as "spiritual" are Christians who have memorized many scriptures and have a working knowledge of the Bible. Believers who are fluent in "Christian lingo," who know doctrine, and who pray well publicly often impress us as being "spiritual." Young believers study their example, anxiously copying their demeanor and speech.

While it's certainly wonderful to know our Bible and Christian doctrine and to be able to pray publicly, these attributes *alone* in no way identify someone as being truly spiritual.

The Two-Fold Test

Remember the Pharisees? They had an incredible command of the Scriptures. The Pharisees knew doctrine backward and forward, and made long public prayers regularly. They were the respected spiritual giants of their day, and Jesus flatly called them *hypocrites!* He warned His disciples, "Beware of the leaven of the Pharisees, which is hypocrisy" (Luke 12:1). The Pharisees had a veneer of spirituality, but inside they were selfish, wretched men.

We would be wrong to assume that men and women who know their Bibles and Christian doctrine and pray well publicly are automatically hypocrites! But we must know that such attributes are at best an incomplete measure of spirituality.

What then is the *true* measure? What makes someone spiritual? The answer is two-fold:

> And He said to him, " 'You shall love the Lord your God with all your heart, and with all your soul, and with all your mind.' This is the great and foremost commandment. The second is like it, 'You shall love your neighbor as yourself.' On these two commandments depend the whole Law and the Prophets"—Matthew 22:37-40.

This scripture sums up our responsibility to God and men and therefore defines true spirituality. We are supposed to love God *and* love our neighbor.

Today's church places a heavy emphasis on our upward call, and rightfully so. Christians flock to seminars on worship and prayer. Local churches expend considerable time and energy to teach people proper doctrine. But what about our duty to our fellow man? Most churches place little or no emphasis on meeting the pressing, practical needs in their locality and abroad.

The following truth seems to have been lost in the shuffle for spiritual greatness:

> Whoever wishes to become great among you shall be your servant; and whoever wishes to be first among you shall be slave of all. For even the

Son of Man did not come to be served, but to
serve, and to give His life a ransom for many—
Mark 10:43-45.

True spiritual greatness is a combination of loving God
and following Christ's example of *loving and serving
people.* Practicing one truth to the exclusion of the other
will cause the church to miss that dynamic balance.

Who is My Neighbor?

One "spiritual giant" in Jesus' day who wanted to justify
his lack of love and service for his fellow man asked the
question, "And who is my neighbor?" (Luke 10:29) We must
ask the same question today: Who is my neighbor? Who are
we responsible to love and serve, and how far should we
go in loving and serving them?

The above-mentioned scripture, "Whoever wishes to
become great shall be *your* servant," reminds us that we have
a special responsibility to take care of our brothers and
sisters in the faith. Both James and John rebuked those who
professed to love God but neglected their brethren:

If a brother or sister is without clothing and in
need of daily food, and one of you says to them,
"Go in peace, be warmed and be filled," and yet
you do not give them what is necessary for their
body, what use is that?—James 2:15,16.

We know love by this, that He laid down His life
for us; and we ought to lay down our lives for
the brethren. But whoever has the world's goods,
and beholds his brother in need and closes his
heart against him, how does the love of God
abide in him? Little children, let us not love with
word or with tongue, but in deed and truth—
1 John 3:16-18.

We must serve fellow Christians in whatever way their need requires. But our duty does not stop there. The Lord commands His disciples to serve those *outside* the faith; those who might not value or appreciate our help—or those who might even despise it. The following passage must be one of the least quoted passages in the Bible:

> And just as you want people to treat you, treat them in the same way. And if you love those who love you, what credit is that to you? For even sinners love those who love them. And if you do good to those who do good to you, what credit is that to you? For even sinners do the same.
>
> And if you lend to those from whom you expect to receive, what credit is that to you? Even sinners lend to sinners, in order to receive back the same amount.
>
> But love your enemies, and do good, and lend, expecting nothing in return; and your reward will be great, and you will be sons of the Most High; for He Himself is kind to ungrateful and evil men—Luke 6:31-35.

Thus, the answer to "Who is my neighbor?" is, *anyone* who is in need, whether sinner or saint. If it is possible for us to help our neighbor, we have an *obligation* to do so.

Our Duty to All Men

The answer to the question, "How far should I go in serving my fellow man?" is critically important here. The current narrow concept of our obligation to the individual sinner or our society usually does not go beyond sharing "the four spiritual laws." The Bible, however, paints a much larger picture of our duty to all men.

> Vindicate the weak and fatherless; do justice to the afflicted and destitute. Rescue the weak and needy; deliver them out of the hand of the wicked—Psalm 82:3,4.

> Speak up for those who cannot speak for themselves, for the rights of all who are destitute. Speak up and judge fairly; defend the rights of the poor and needy—Proverbs 31:8,9, NIV.

We are commanded to secure justice for the weak, the afflicted, the destitute, the needy, and the fatherless. The Bible speaks of our obligation toward the alien, the orphan, the widow, and the needy.

> At the end of every third year you shall bring out all the tithe of your produce in that year, and shall deposit it in your town . . . and the alien, the orphan and the widow who are in your town, shall come and eat and be satisfied, in order that the Lord your God may bless you in all the work of your hand which you do—Deuteronomy 14:28,29.

> For the Lord your God is the God of gods and the Lord of lords, the great, the mighty, and the awesome God who does not show partiality, nor take a bribe. He executes justice for the orphan and the widow, and shows His love for the alien by giving him food and clothing. So show your love for the alien, for you were aliens in the land of Egypt—Deuteronomy 10:17-19.

Our love for the alien—those outside of the faith—is shown by providing the needy among them with food and clothing.

These scriptures are commands, not suggestions. But who is actually fulfilling these commands? Is the Department of Social Services doing the church's job because we have failed to be obedient?

Pure Religion in God's Sight

Some would argue that since these passages are in the Old Testament they do not apply to us. Being spiritual today, they say, does not include meeting individual and social needs. Why then did James give the following injunction?

> This is pure and undefiled religion in the sight of our God and Father, to visit orphans and widows in their distress, and to keep oneself unstained by the world—James 1:27.

This New Testament command sums up the scriptures quoted in the Old Testament. The meaning of this scripture is not that we stop by the orphanage or the retirement home and pay a visit. According to *Strong's Concordance* the Greek word for "visit" is *episkeptomai*. The word means to inspect, to go to see, and to relieve. Matthew Henry in his commentary explains it this way:

> Visiting is here put for all manner of relief which we are capable of giving to others; and fatherless and widows are here particularly mentioned, because they are generally most apt to be neglected or oppressed; but by them, we are to clearly understand all who are proper objects of charity, all who are in affliction. It is very remarkable that if the sum of religion be drawn up in two articles, this is one—to be charitable and relieve the afflicted.

To be truly spiritual, or "religious" in the good sense, we must deliberately seek out the fatherless and the widow (among others) and relieve their distress in any way we can. In the Golden Rule, the Lord summed up our responsibility to all men in one simple sentence. "Therefore, however you want people to treat you, so treat them, for this is the Law and the Prophets" (Matthew 7:12).

The next time you study your Bible, use a concordance to look up verses containing words like justice, judgment, rescue, deliver, vindicate, innocent, needy, weak, fatherless, and widow. You will find an overwhelming number of verses commanding *action* from God's people on behalf of the needy. The verses already mentioned are not isolated exceptions, but the rule.

Out of the Saltshaker

In order to obey many of these scriptures, we will have to leave the comfort and safety of our church pews. We are going to have to get our hands dirty, and be *active* in our society. That is why James 1:27 says "This is pure and undefiled religion in the sight of our God and Father, to visit orphans and widows in their distress, and *to keep oneself unstained by the world."*

If Christians stay cloistered in their little groups, it's easy to keep unstained by the world. But when we go to the trenches of this life, when we reach out to help the unlovely, we run the risk of being defiled. Involving yourself in society, rather than abandoning it, presents a far greater challenge to stay pure.

Jesus said, "You are the salt of the earth" (Matthew 5:13). Salt was primarily used as a preservative and also for medicinal purposes. Christians who get involved in society can preserve righteousness and help heal what is wrong.

The Lord went on to say, "But if the salt has become tasteless, how will it be made salty again? It is good for nothing anymore, except to be thrown out and trampled under foot by men." By misinterpreting 2 Corinthians 6:17 ("Therefore, come out from their midst and be separate"), many have neglected their God-given commands to influence society and serve their fellow man.

When salt (the Christian influence) stops preserving a nation, that society is going to deteriorate. There's no way around it.

Confronting Political Leaders

Seeking justice and reform will inevitably thrust us into the political arena. This is not new for God's people. His messengers often had to confront and challenge political leaders with His righteous precepts.

Isaiah prophesied against the lawmakers of his day,

> "Woe to those who enact evil statutes, and to those who constantly record unjust decisions, so as to deprive the needy of justice, and rob the poor of My people of their rights, in order that widows may be their spoil, and that they may plunder the orphans"—Isaiah 10:1,2.

Jeremiah demanded justice from Judah's leaders. God instructed him to proclaim this message in the king's palace:

> "Hear the word of the Lord, O king of Judah, you who sit on David's throne—you, your officials and your people who come through these gates. This is what the Lord says: Do what is just and right. Rescue from the hand of his oppressor the one who has been robbed. Do no wrong or violence to the alien, the fatherless or the widow, and do not shed innocent blood in this place"— Jeremiah 22:2,3, NIV.

He then gave a scathing rebuke to Jehoiakim:

> "Do you become a king because you are compet-
> ing in cedar? Did not your father eat and drink,
> and do justice and righteousness? Then it was well
> with him. He pled the cause of the afflicted and
> needy; then it was well. Is not that what it means
> to know Me?" declares the Lord. "But your eyes
> and your heart are intent only upon your own
> dishonest gain, and on shedding innocent blood
> and on practicing oppression and extortion"—
> Jeremiah 22:15-17.

These rebukes are not vague, they are clear. Isaiah and
Jeremiah both pointed out *specific* evils that *specific* rulers
were involved in, and identified the individuals who were
suffering.

Does It Apply to America?

Some would argue that Israel's historical lessons are not
applicable to America because Israel was a theocracy in
covenant with God. They argue that God does not command
non-covenant nations and their leaders to change their ways
and their laws in the same way He spoke to Israel.

Why then do we have the books of Jonah, Nahum, and
Obadiah? All three prophecies were to heathen nations. Why
does Scripture contain passages in the books of Amos,
Jeremiah, and Isaiah, which are also prophecies and
commands to non-covenant nations? Because God is "the
God of all flesh" (Jeremiah 32:27).

We err if we think that God does not demand even
heathen nations to obey Him. He does. If God did not require
all nations to obey His Law, He would have no basis by which
to judge them for their sin. For without the Law, there is
no knowledge of sin. (See Romans 3:20.)

We must follow the prophet's example and take the Word and precepts of our God into America's political spectrum. We must confront legislators and judges with their injustice. We must also challenge others in positions of power—such as the media elite, hospital boards, university boards, and school boards—when their laws, policies, and biases permit or endorse that which is against God's law.

Beyond that, members of our church should run for political office and seek to hold jobs and positions where policies are made and public opinion is formed. This may create a stir in the media, to put it mildly.

What Should We Expect?

Some courageous Christian leaders, stepping into the lion's den of politics to address today's critical issues, have been met with bared fangs. This should not surprise us. On the contrary, we should expect it!

Jesus *promised* that the world would hate us as we confront the evil in it. (See John 15:18-21). In fact, He even testified of Himself, "The world . . . hates Me, because I testify of it, that its deeds are evil" (John 7:7).

Jesus also gave us these words of comfort: "Blessed are those who have been persecuted for the sake of righteousness, for theirs is the kingdom of heaven" (Matthew 5:10). This verse could be paraphrased, "Blessed are those who have been persecuted for standing up for what is right, for theirs is the kingdom of heaven."

Jesus went on to say, "Blessed are you when men cast insults at you, and persecute you, and say all kinds of evil against you falsely, on account of Me. Rejoice, and be glad, for your reward in heaven is great, for so they persecuted the prophets who were before you" (Matthew 5:11,12).

Wouldn't it be nice if the makers of Christian "promise" cards and devotionals would include some of these *promises* of persecution!

A High Calling

We should not be discouraged when standing for truth and righteousness brings us persecutions and false accusations. We should *rejoice!*

What revival would take place if the churches were filled with joyful testimonies of Christians being persecuted for standing for what is right! What glory would be given to God if His children did not run from situations that bring persecution! What pleasure God would take in His people if they stopped thinking they must be doing something *wrong* if they are hated.

The fact is, we are probably doing something wrong if we are *not* persecuted. The apostle Paul declared, "Everyone who wants to live a godly life in Christ Jesus will be persecuted, while evil men and imposters will go from bad to worse, deceiving and being deceived" (2 Timothy 3:12,13 NIV).

Those who come under and endure persecution and reviling have the high privilege of being compared with prophets like Jeremiah, Isaiah, and Ezekiel. But when we follow the example of the prophets, we can expect some of their earthly reward—trouble!

Jeremiah's twenty-seven year denunciation of social evils in Judah and God's impending judgment brought him isolation from family and friends, and at least one beating. He was confined in stocks, his life was threatened, and he was finally imprisoned.

Fortunately, other men and women of God have handed us a legacy of hope that an evil and godless society can be changed. In Nineveh, a non-covenant nation, everyone from the king to the peasants responded to Jonah's message, and God spared that great city.

Deborah's ministry not only produced repentance, but a tremendous victory against an oppressive army (See Judges 4 and 5). When Gideon tore down the idol in his father's yard, God used him and a band of three hundred men to route a massive Midianite army. (See Judges 6 and 7).

As we take an active role in molding our society and reaching out to individuals in need, we will inevitably have a good, "salty" effect. The needy will be benefited, and the wrongs will be made right. When the apostle Paul and Silas went to Thessalonica, the welcoming committee said, "These men who have turned the world upside down have come here also" (Acts 17:6).

A Mandate, Not an Option

Social responsibilities are not an *option* for God's people. They are a *mandate.* Our religious lives and ceremonies may be flowing nicely, but if we neglect our fellow man, God is not pleased with our spiritual gymnastics.

Isaiah's prophesy against Israel is a perfect example. They were faithful to execute the "religious" duties God ordained, but had miserably failed to serve and defend their fellow human beings. God said,

> "What are your multiplied sacrifices to Me? . . .
> I have had enough of burnt offerings of rams, and
> the fat of fed cattle. And I take no pleasure in the
> blood of bulls, lambs, or goats.
>
> "When you come to appear before Me, who
> requires of you this trampling of My courts? Bring
> your worthless offerings no longer, incense is an
> abomination to Me.
>
> "New moon and sabbath, the calling of
> assemblies—I cannot endure iniquity and the
> solemn assembly. I hate your new moon festivals
> and your appointed feasts, they have become a
> burden to Me. I am weary of bearing them.
>
> "So when you spread out your hands in prayer,
> I will hide my eyes from you. Yes, even though

you multiply prayers, I will not listen. Your hands are full of bloodshed.

"Wash yourselves, make yourselves clean; remove the evil of your deeds from My sight. Cease to do evil, learn to do good; seek justice, reprove the ruthless; defend the orphan, plead for the widow"—Isaiah 1:11-18.

Solemn assemblies, burnt offerings, incense, prayers, new moon festivals, and appointed feasts were all commanded *by God*. And the people were very faithful to their religious obligations. But, they were failing to have a righteous effect on the whole of society.

Individuals whom they could have helped were suffering. Because of this neglect, God *hated* their religious motions. They were a stench in His nostrils, *even though He had ordained them*.

Why No Revival?

Today, God's people are often deeply involved in the "religious" activities that God instituted, but are neglecting the "social" responsibilities that God also commanded. Therefore, God is not pleased. This undoubtedly accounts for much of the deadness in many evangelical churches. The religious experience is shallow and self-centered because it neglects "true religion"—namely, helping the fatherless and the widow. (See James 1:27).

No wonder we have not yet seen true revival in our nation. No wonder the church no longer shines as "the light of the world." We have not done what God told us to do.

God's Word makes it clear what He expects from His people and the spiritual renewal that will result from obedience to His commands. Religious exercises like fasting do not impress God when children are being ruthlessly killed and mothers are being maimed; when the poor and hungry are abandoned.

"Is this not the kind of fasting I have chosen:
to loose the chains of injustice and untie the cords
of the yoke, to set the oppressed free, and break
every yoke?

"Is it not to share your food with the hungry
and to provide the poor wanderer with shelter—
when you see the naked, to clothe him, and not
to turn away from your own flesh and blood? . . .

"If you do away with the yoke of oppression,
with the pointing finger and malicious talk, and
if you spend yourselves on behalf of the hungry
and satisfy the needs of the oppressed, then your
light will rise in the darkness, and your night will
become like the noonday"—Isaiah 58:6-10, NIV.

That's the secret to true revival for *any* nation.

Do Something!

Revival will not come by talking about it or even by
preaching against the wickedness of our society.

Detesting the social problems that are destroying our
nation is not enough. Discussing the evils of abortion, infanticide, euthanasia, pornography, and the elimination of the
Christian witness in the public schools is not enough. To
sympathetically listen to pastors thunder their abhorrence
of these atrocities from their pulpits is not enough.

We must *do* something about these evils.

America's cancer can be cured. What is the remedy? Our
obedience to the *whole* Word of God.

Learn to do good; seek justice, reprove the ruthless; defend the orphan, plead for the widow—
Isaiah 1:16.

We must go out from our cloistered groups, into the public arena, and there reprove the ruthless, do justice, and help the fatherless and the widow in their distress. As we do, God will honor our obedience to His commands, and we will begin to see a restoration of righteousness in the market place, the political spectrum, the medical profession, the arts, the media, the universities, the sciences, and the schools.

If we do not obey, I fear God will let America collapse on herself.

——— 4 ———
Robbed of Our Heritage

Rediscovering the Church's
Legacy of Christian Activism

4

Robbed of Our Heritage

Rediscovering the Church's Legacy of Christian Activism

We've been robbed.

"Robbed of what?" you might ask.

Robbed of our heritage!

In the last chapter we learned that God calls Christians to social activism. Our spiritual forefathers left us some shining examples of service to our fellow man. But their examples have been largely forgotten or ignored. Why?

Because most American Christians, especially pastors and seminary professors, have been deceived by the "I'm only called to preach the gospel" mentality. ("Gospel" meaning a gospel of personal salvation—an escape from hell.) Christians in our nation have forgotten or deliberately ignored the justice and service our forefathers rendered to the needy and oppressed.

Saints like Moody, Finney, Spurgeon, Amy Carmichael, and others are studied only for their "soul-winning efforts," while their social activism is quietly ignored. Granted, their evangelistic endeavors were great, but the expression of their Christianity went far beyond saving lost souls. *They were activists.*

The biographies of these great men and women of God show that they met people where their physical need was greatest and *satisfied* it. Perhaps they were so successful in "spiritual endeavors" because they labored tirelessly in "earthly endeavors." The ultimate was won as the immediate was conquered.

Let's examine recent church history and the tremendous legacy of Christian activism that godly men and women left for our generation. Focusing on their lives will paint a more accurate portrait of evangelistic fervor mixed with hard work for the needy and oppressed, a balance desperately needed today.

Meeting Temporal and Spiritual Needs

The most famous evangelist of the nineteenth century was Dwight L. Moody. He was born in 1837 on a Northfield, Massachusetts farm and converted to Christ in 1856 while living in Boston selling shoes for his uncle. A few years later, he went to Chicago to make his fortune in the shoe business, but before long the call of God emerged triumphant over Moody's desire to become rich.

His massive evangelistic campaigns took him throughout America and England where thousands of people were brought to a saving knowledge of Christ and planted in local churches. Granted, many who went to "inquiry rooms" did not follow through with any commitment, but nonetheless, many did. By Moody's spoken and printed word, millions heard the gospel.

Moody's compassion caused him to reach out to meet people's temporal as well as spiritual needs. When visiting with his brother Samuel in Northfield, they were riding in a carriage and passed a lonely little cottage.

Sitting in the doorway were the mother and two daughters, occupied in braiding straw hats. The father was paralytic, and could do nothing for the support of the family; thus the burden rested on the women. But though the father was physically helpless, he was an educated man, and his daughters had an ambition that reached beyond their present narrow horizon.

The limitations of their condition and apparent hopelessness of their future deeply impressed Mr. Moody. The sight of those women braiding hats in that lonely, out-of-the-way place resulted in his determination to meet the peculiar needs of just such girls in neighboring hills and communities.[1]

In the spring of 1879, ground was broken for a hall capable of holding one hundred students. Moody, as was characteristic, could not wait for a dormitory to be constructed, so he altered his own home and opened the school with eight female students in mind. Instead, twenty-five arrived! Among these twenty-five young ladies were the two Moody had seen outside the cottage that fateful day.

Northfield Schools

Over the next several years, the school grew to encompass over five hundred acres of land, which housed over twenty buildings. They included a library, an auditorium, a gymnasium, a bookstore, several barns, and nine dormitories, along with the Moodys' personal residence. Almost four hundred students *per year* enrolled in this awesome complex by the turn of the century.

Soon after the girls' school was opened, plans for a similar institution for young men were under way. In November 1879, Mr. Moody secured a farm of one hundred and seventy-five acres, also in Northfield, and then an adjoining farm of one hundred acres. In 1881, Mt. Hermon School was opened in the two farmhouses.

The enrollment of Mt. Hermon, like the Seminary, grew to about four hundred men. Non-Christians were admitted. Tuition was not free, but very low, so no one would be denied the opportunity of learning. The curriculum was flexible enough to accommodate young men even if they had no prior scholastic exposure.

> In both these Northfield schools, the end in view has been to impart knowledge, not so much as an accomplishment, but as a means of making men and women more serviceable to society.[2]

Moody understood that he could affect the moral fabric of the nation as he helped mold the lives of men and women, most of whom were *not* going into what we commonly refer to as "the ministry." But doubtless they were the "salt of the earth" wherever they were scattered. Shouldn't exemplifying the life of Christ and having an effect on society be considered "ministry"?

India's Dark Secret

Scarcely has the world known a saint of the caliber of Amy Carmichael. Her rich devotional life and her sacrificial work have inspired countless Christians. This beautiful young woman laid down her life for India's children, and the work she began continues to this day.

In 1895, after having served the poor of her Irish homeland, Amy Carmichael landed on Indian soil, where she remained until she went to her eternal home in 1951. She went to India with the thought of evangelizing the Indians for Christ, which she did. But before long, she discovered India's evil, dark secret: child selling for child prostitution. This wicked trade was hidden inside the dark Hindu temples that filled South India.

On March 9, 1901, Amy was awakened to the horror of these temples. A little seven-year-old girl named Pearleyes, who had recently been given to the temple by her mother, miraculously escaped. Providence had Amy stop at the house where the child had fled, and there little Pearleyes opened Amy's eyes to the secrets of hell.

Broken Jewels

The famous Ghandi testified that many of these "temples" were no better than brothels. Actually, they were far worse, for many involved sexual exploitation of girls nine, eight, and even five years old.

The temples secured little girls in a number of ways—the first of which was religious deception. In many Hindu minds, it was a station of honor for a young girl to be "married" to a god. This often made the parents deliberately blind to the heartwrenching degradation to which their daughter would be subjected.

Sometimes when the firstborn was a girl, the parents would give their daughter to a temple hoping that the gods would be pleased and their next child would be a boy. Or if the mother died, the father would sometimes give the girl (whether an infant or five years old) to the temple to save the expense and trouble of hiring a nurse to care for the girl. If the father died, the mother might sell a daughter to a temple to relieve financial hardship.

By whatever means, or for whatever reason, little girls were being imprisoned in these temples to lives of unthinkable immorality. The inner cries of their consciences against such vileness were slowly silenced by continual instruction in unclean thought, art, and deeds. Having been brainwashed and worn down in her thinking, a young girl eventually believed her practice to be honorable and right. Venereal disease claimed the lives of many of these broken jewels who were so young they should have still been playing with dolls.

Rescuing Children

Into this nightmare walked Amy Carmichael. While many missionaries were ignorant or indifferent to the plight of the children, God gripped her heart with an anguish and burden for these little girls that directed the rest of her life.

Amy began seeking inroads into this trade in children, but met with blank stares, closed mouths, and stone walls.

> Wherever we went after that day, we were constrained to gather facts about what appeared a great secret: traffic in the souls and bodies of young children, and we search for some way to save them, and we could find no way. The helpless little things seemed to slip between our fingers as we stretched out our hands to grasp them, or it was as though a great wave swept up and carried them out to sea. In a kind of desperation, we sought for a way. But we found that we must know more before we could hope to find it.[3]

After much time, prayer, anguish of heart, and hard work, a door into this underworld began to open. Three infants, all scheduled to be dedicated to temples, were secured by Amy and her Indian co-workers. Elation was followed by heartbreak when all three infants died of disease within a year. Despite her disappointment, Miss Carmichael continued in God's burden for these children.

> Things are sure to happen which will drain the heart of human hope, but the hallmark of the true missionary (the good Lord make it ours) is refusal to be weakened or hardened or soured or made hopeless by disappointment.[4]

Thank God, more children were rescued, and Amy started Dohnavur Fellowship, with the objective of saving little girls and later little boys from dedication to the temples of demons. A bag was always packed, and cash on hand for her or one of her co-workers to travel hundreds or even a thousand miles to attempt to rescue a child.

Dohnavur Fellowship

What began in a single home with a few sisters in the Lord and several small children, grew into a glorious testimony of Christian love in action. In 1907, Mabel Wade, a registered nurse, joined the mission. More children were rescued. Nursery age children grew to school age children, and a school was constructed. In 1909, three teachers from Europe were added to the ministry. The children were taught to read and write, to love hard work, and to serve the Lord with gladness by serving their fellow man.

By 1923, Dohnavur Fellowship had thirty nurseries! In 1929, over seven hundred boys, girls, and Christian workers lived at this thriving community. By 1938, the complex covered over one hundred and seventy acres, consisting of nurseries, workshops, a boys' compound, a girls' compound, a weaving room, a school, and a power house (for electricity).

That same year, another miracle was added: "The Place of Heavenly Healing," a hospital complete with medical staff, which provided care not only for the saints at Dohnavur, but also for the surrounding villages. This hospital opened a glorious door to share the gospel with the lost.

Results Not Reputation

God used this precious woman to rescue children from temple prostitution, then trained them to serve their own people. As a result of the upheaval and attention Amy Carmichael brought to this hideous trade, child prostitution was eventually made illegal in India. Her work had a lasting effect and continues to this day.

Looking back, we can see the beauty of God in her work. But as always, many of her contemporaries questioned much of what she did. She endured much misunderstanding for her obedience to God. Some missionaries thought she was off base. But she persevered, looking to the day she would see her Savior face to face. This following quote expresses the steadfastness of her heart:

> The work was to develop upon lines that would not find general acceptance, and we had to learn the unchangeable truth: our Master has never promised us success. He demands obedience. He expects faithfulness. Results are His concern, not ours. And our reputation is a matter of no consequence at all.[5]

Her life was a constant testimony because she lived out these words. May God grant us more saints half the caliber of Amy Carmichael.

Ministering to Widows and Orphans

Charles Haddon Spurgeon is affectionately remembered as the "Prince of preachers," a title earned by his unmatched oratorical beauty in preaching Christ and expounding the Scriptures. Literally thousands in England were converted to Christ through his ministry. Spurgeon's fame and influence as a minister of the gospel spread to several continents through the distribution of his sermons and books.

Some in his position might be "so heavenly minded, they're no earthly good." Not so with Spurgeon. He had a deep desire to better the social conditions that existed in England. Unfortunately, that aspect of his ministry has been largely ignored or forgotten.

Spurgeon entered the ministry at the tender age of seventeen and two years later accepted an invitation to become the pastor of the New Park Street Baptist Church in London. When he arrived, the church had been underwriting a home for elderly women. A few years later, Spurgeon built a more modern facility closer to the church, called the "Almshouses." Seventeen small homes were jointly built, where these elderly women were provided with shelter, food, clothing, and spending money.

Free government education did not exist in Spurgeon's day. Ever concerned that people should learn to read and write, Spurgeon built a school adjoining the Almshouses that could teach nearly four hundred children. For several years, Spurgeon paid for the light, heat, and other expenses out of his own pocket.

At that time, London had tens of thousands of orphans wandering her streets. Poorly clothed and incredibly dirty, they escaped starvation by eating whatever they could find in the garbage or could steal. Most were destined for an early grave or the jails.

A New Work

One evening at a prayer meeting in the summer of 1866, Spurgeon challenged his people saying, "Dear friends, we are a huge church, and should be doing more for the Lord in this great city. I want us, tonight, to ask him to send us some new work; and if we need money to carry it on, let us pray that the means also may be sent."[6]

A few days later, Mrs. Hillyard, a woman unknown to Spurgeon, wrote him about her desire to donate twenty thousand pounds (a sum today equalling several million dollars) for the care and instruction of orphan boys. God answered their prayer for a "new work," and they joyously began to provide for children in need.

Unlike other "institutions" that typically had a large dormitory and mess hall, this huge, beautiful complex was a deliberately "home-like" series of houses. Each house

held fourteen boys and one matron, who was like a mother
to them. Later a series of houses for orphan girls was erected.
These destitute children came from various religious back-
grounds. Many were converted to Christ; others were not.
But all who came were provided a loving home and a good
education.

The Metropolitan Tabernacle

When Spurgeon's congregation experienced tremendous
growth, plans were drawn up for a new church, "The
Metropolitan Tabernacle," which seated three thousand six
hundred, and had standing room for another two thousand.
When the new church was completed and in full operation,
it became the center of an astounding amount of activity—
the doors were open from seven in the morning to eleven
at night.

The Metropolitan Tabernacle ministered to the most pressing needs in their community. Where illiteracy contributed
to the cycle of poverty and prevented men from becoming
better providers for their families, night classes were offered
to teach the basic skills of reading and writing. Mathematics
and shorthand were also offered.

Several societies were organized to meet practical needs.
The Ladies' Benevolent Society had "sewing circles" to make
clothes for the orphans, the poor of the church, and other
poor people in the area. The Maternal Society prepared gifts
for expectant mothers, then assisted with household chores
after the women gave birth. The Flower Society made
beautiful bouquets and baskets for the sick. They delivered
these seeds of cheer to those sick at home or in the hospital.

The recipients of the practical outreaches of Spurgeon's
work were *not* limited to the flock of God. Whether food,
clothing, education, a home, or flowers, these rays of care
shone on all the British people, especially the poor.

By the preaching of the gospel, teaching people to read,
write, and add, taking care of the orphans and widows,

training young ministers, and providing clothing for the poor, all of England, especially London, felt the impact of Charles Haddon Spurgeon and the Metropolitan Tabernacle.

Meeting the Need of the Hour

I have deliberately looked at the lives of Moody, Spurgeon, and Amy Carmichael because they are often remembered for only their soul winning efforts or gifted preaching. Ignoring their acts of mercy, as many have done, reveals a bias *against* social activism in American Christianity.

Some would rather rewrite church history and cast spiritual giants of the past as being pietists, solely concerned with evangelism and the hereafter, than to admit the gross deficiency that exists in the church today. Whether they ministered to the poor, fed the hungry, built hospitals, or rescued infants from the horrors of child prostitution, these Christians based their actions on a solid biblical foundation.

A common thread binds these great saints. Whatever a fellow human being needed at the time, they provided. The hungry were fed; the naked were clothed; the homeless were taken in; and the oppressed were defended. God's servants rose up to meet the need of the hour.

Throughout the world, Christians have founded hospitals, schools, orphanages, universities, and organizations that serve people at the point of their need. All these acts of mercy were a testimony to lost men that Christ is real. That's why Christ commanded, "Let your light shine before men in such a way that they may see your *good works,* and glorify your Father who is in heaven (Matthew 5:16, italics added).

The Needs of Our Generation

Our generation faces immense needs of its own. For example, a cocaine rehabilitation center would have been unnecessary two hundred years ago. But today, thousands of young lives are being devastated by drug abuse. In response to the crisis, Teen Challenge was born. Young men and women, who are often in trouble with the law as a result of their addictions, can seek rehabilitation at one of the Teen Challenge centers.

These centers house ten to twenty young people and are staffed with trained Christian workers. From there, many young men go on to "The Farm" in Pennsylvania, where they attend classes in Bible and English, learn self-discipline, and are taught a trade such as printing, carpentry, or auto mechanics.

The most crushing need facing the church today is to rescue children and mothers from the abortion holocaust. Homes for unwed mothers are emerging as bright spots in the dark blight of abortion that covers our nation. In response to skyrocketing teenage pregnancies, godly chastity programs teaching sexual purity are growing to stem the tide of fornication. As an alternative to abortion, Christian houses of mercy are being opened to reach out to young women in need.

Many children have been saved from death, young women have been spared the nightmare of abortion, and many have been won to Christ. Some homes offer continuance of education and/or some vocational training, and all young women learn the basics of mothering. Some young mothers choose to place their child for adoption with Christian parents. Whatever the case, the presence of these homes is an oasis in the midst of a desert of contemporary Christian social activism.

You Did It to Me

Jesus said that He would separate the sheep from the goats. His judgment at that time will be based solely on one criteria—*action*. What about those who didn't do anything wrong—they just didn't do anything? According to Jesus, *inaction* would be considered disobedience and apathy toward the Savior. Sympathy is not taken into account, nor are prayers, such as "be warmed and be filled" (James 2:16), but only concrete, practical actions for those in need.

> Then the King will say to those on His right, "Come, you who are blessed of my Father, inherit the kingdom prepared for you from the foundation of the world. For I was hungry and you gave Me something to eat; I was thirsty, and you gave Me drink; I was a stranger and you invited Me in; naked, and you clothed Me; I was sick, and you visited Me; I was in prison, and you came to Me."
>
> Then the righteous will answer Him, saying, "Lord, when did we see You hungry, and feed You, or thirsty, and give You drink? And when did we see You a stranger, and invite You in, or naked, and clothe You? And when did we see You sick, or in prison, and come to You?"
>
> And the King will answer and say to them, "Truly I say to you, to the extent that you did it to one of these brothers of Mine, even the least of them, you did it to Me"—Matthew 25:34-40.

Some people want to argue about who are the "least of Christ's brethren." *Whoever* they are, be it the church, Israel, the poor, the lost, or children, the point is this—the judgment of the sheep and goats revolves around their *actions* for those suffering and in need.

How will this generation of American Christians fare at the judgment seat of Christ?

Across our country thousands of believers are peacefully blockading so-called "women's health clinics" to bring an end to the slaughter of innocent babies. They realize that to do nothing is a sin against Christ.

These Christians will not—in fact, they cannot—ignore the need of the hour. With Christ's words burning in their hearts, they want to be able to look Jesus in the face and hear Him say, "When you rescued the unborn, you rescued Me."

5
Higher Laws

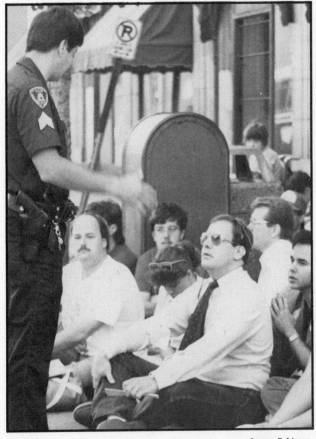

Jeanne Robinson

Should We Obey God Rather Than Men?

5

Higher Laws

Should We Obey God Rather Than Men?

There's an old saying, "He who frames the question wins the debate." It's true.

If I asked, "Should Christians break the law?" most Christians would quickly answer *"No!"*

However, if I reframed the question, "Should Christians obey God's Word even if it means disobeying the ungodly laws of men?" many believers would say "Yes." Others wouldn't know what to do!

Christians who insist we should never break man's law quickly quote the injunctions of Romans 13:1-5 and 1 Peter 2:13-15 to obey civil authority. Let's look at those passages.

> Let every person be in subjection to the governing authorities. For there is no authority except from God, and those which exist are established by God.
>
> Therefore he who resists authority has opposed the ordinance of God; and they who have opposed will receive condemnation upon themselves. For rulers are not a cause of fear for good behavior, but for evil.

Do you want to have no fear of authority? Do what is good, and you will have praise from the same; for it is a minister of God to you for good. But if you do what is evil, be afraid; for it does not bear the sword for nothing; for it is a minister of God, an avenger who brings wrath upon the one who practices evil.

Wherefore it is necessary to be in subjection, not only because of wrath, but also for conscience' sake—Romans 13:1-5.

Submit yourselves for the Lord's sake to every human institution, whether to a king as the one in authority, or to governors as sent by him for the punishment of evildoers and the praise of those who do right.

For such is the will of God that by doing right you may silence the ignorance of foolish men— 1 Peter 2:13-15.

These passages obviously teach that we *should* respect and obey civil authority. In fact, Christians should be the *most* law-abiding citizens in the country.

But should a Christian *ever* disobey civil authority, especially when civil authority asks us to ignore and disobey the clear teachings of God's Word? Fortunately, Scripture is not silent on that issue. Numerous Old and New Testament passages shed some startling light on our responsibility in such a conflict. Let's carefully examine several such instances.

Kill the Newborns!

During the days of Israel's sojourning in Egypt, Jews were growing so numerous that the Egyptians began to view them as a possible military threat. To quell this potential danger, the Egyptians forced the Israelites to become slaves. To further curb Israel's growth, Pharaoh devised a wicked plot to kill Israel's newborn children. Here is the account of that plot, and the story of two courageous women.

> Then the king of Egypt spoke to the Hebrew midwives, one of whom was named Shiphrah, and the other was named Puah; and he said, "When you are helping the Hebrew women to give birth and see them upon the birthstool, if it is a son, then you shall put him to death; but if it is a daughter, then she shall live."
> But the midwives feared God, and did not do as the king of Egypt had commanded them, but let the boys live.
> So the king of Egypt called for the midwives, and said to them, "Why have you done this thing, and let the boys live?"
> And the midwives said to Pharaoh, "Because the Hebrew women are not as the Egyptian women; for they are vigorous, and they give birth before the midwife can get to them."
> So God was good to the midwives, and the people multiplied, and became very mighty. And it came about because the midwives feared God, that He established households for them—Exodus 1:15-21.

This was a courageous act of obedience to God. Because God was pleased with their disobedience to the king's command, He blessed the midwives with large families.

Why Did the Midwives Lie?

Remember that the king's *word* was *law* in those days. Therefore, disobeying the word of a king *was* breaking the law. "I say, 'Keep the command of the king because of the oath before God. . . . Since the word of the king is authoritative, who will say to him, 'What are you doing?' " (Ecclesiastes 8:2,4).

The concept of a constitutional republic or a democracy—a legislative body elected by the people who in turn made laws—was non-existent. Breaking the word of the king was the same as breaking a law passed by legislators in America, with one frightening difference: "The wrath of the king is as messengers of death" (Proverbs 16:14).

When someone disobeyed the king, they put their life in jeopardy. The Bible records many instances where a man was put to death for displeasing a king. That would explain why the midwives, along with Moses' parents and Rahab, used some deception or trickery in their heroism. They feared for their lives.

Not Afraid of the King's Edict

The second example of obeying God rather than man is Moses' parents. When Pharaoh saw that his original plan to secretly kill male Hebrew children failed, he issued a more barbaric decree.

> Then Pharaoh commanded all his people, saying, "Every son who is born you are to cast into the Nile, and every daughter you are to keep alive."
> Now a man from the house of Levi went and married a daughter of Levi. And the woman conceived and bore a son; and when she saw that he was beautiful, she hid him for three months. But when she could hide him no longer, she got him a wicker basket and covered it over with tar and pitch. Then she put the child into it, and set it among the reeds by the bank of the Nile. And his sister stood at a distance to find out what would happen to him.

Then the daughter of Pharaoh came down to bathe at the Nile, with her maidens walking alongside the Nile; and she saw the basket among the reeds and sent her maid, and she brought it to her. When she opened it, she saw the child, and behold, the boy was crying. And she had pity on him and said, "This is one of the Hebrews' children."

Then his sister said to Pharaoh's daughter, "Shall I go and call a nurse for you from the Hebrew women, that she may nurse the child for you?" And Pharaoh's daughter said to her, "Go ahead." So the girl went and called the child's mother.

Then Pharaoh's daughter said to her, "Take this child away and nurse him for me and I shall give you your wages." So the woman took the child and nursed him. And the child grew, and she brought him to Pharaoh's daughter, and he became her son. And she named him Moses, and said, "Because I drew him out of the water"— Exodus 1:22-2:10.

Referring to this event, Hebrews 11:23 says, "By faith Moses, when he was born, was hidden for three months by his parents, because they saw he was a beautiful child; and they were not afraid of the king's edict."

Moses' parents act of "civil disobedience" saved the life of their son, and catapulted them into the "Faith Hall of Fame." God *expected* Moses' parents to disobey the king, and He blessed them for their actions. The baby boy they saved from death grew up to become one of the greatest men, not only of the Bible, but of all time.

Treason Against the King

After wandering in the desert for forty years, the Israelites were about to enter the inheritance God promised them. Possibly to avoid a duplication of the bad report given by the ten spies, only two spies were sent to preview the land ahead of Joshua and the armies of Israel. Here is the account of their adventure, and their deliverance from what seemed certain death.

> Then Joshua the son of Nun sent two men as spies secretly from Shittim, saying, "Go, view the land, especially Jericho." So they went and came into the house of a harlot whose name was Rahab, and lodged there.
>
> And it was told the king of Jericho, saying, "Behold, men from the sons of Israel have come here tonight to search out the land."
>
> And the king of Jericho sent word to Rahab, saying, "Bring out the men who have come to you, who have entered your house, for they have come to search out the land."
>
> But the woman had taken the two men and hidden them, and she said, "Yes, the men came to me, but I did not know where they were from. And it came about when it was time to shut the gate, at dark, that the men went out; I do not know where the men went. Pursue them quickly, for you will overtake them."
>
> But she had brought them up to the roof and hidden them in the stalks of flax which she had laid in order on the roof. . . . Then she let them down by a rope through the window, for her house was on the city wall—Joshua 2:1-6,15.

Rahab had a choice. She could obey the command of the king and turn over the spies, or she could obey the voice of God in her heart and hide them; treason against the king or treason against God. Because she believed that the God of Israel was the only God and was to be obeyed before the king, she disobeyed the king's command.

Rahab risked her life to protect the spies, siding with the people of Israel and obeying their great God. God honored her obedience to Himself by sparing her and her family during the conquest of Jericho. They were the *only* survivors. Rahab became one of the heroines of faith (see Hebrews 11:31), and beyond that, she is part of the Messianic lineage mentioned in Christ's genealogy (see Matthew 1:5).

We Won't Worship Your Idols!

After the conquest of Jerusalem by Nebuchadnezzar, three young noblemen named Shadrach, Meshach, and Abed-nego found themselves among the Jewish captives in Babylon. While serving as advisors to the king, they were faced with a choice: obey the king by bowing down to worship the golden idol he set up (see Daniel 3:5,6) or obey God who said, "You shall fear only the Lord your God; and you shall worship Him, and swear by His name. You shall not follow other gods, any of the gods of the peoples who surround you" (Deuteronomy 6:13,14).

The exciting account of their courageous stand has become one of the most popular Sunday school stories of all time. How did the king respond to the charges brought against these Hebrews who refused to commit idolatry?

> Then Nebuchadnezzar in rage and anger gave orders to bring Shadrach, Meshach and Abed-nego; then these men were brought before the king.
>
> Nebuchadnezzar responded and said to them, "Is it true, Shadrach, Meshach and Abed-nego, that you do not serve my gods or worship the golden image that I have set up? Now if you are ready . . . to fall down and worship the image that I have made, very well. But if you will not worship, you will immediately be cast into the midst of a furnace of blazing fire; and what god is there who can deliver you out of my hands?"

> Shadrach, Meshach and Abed-nego answered and said to the king, "O Nebuchadnezzar, we do not need to give you an answer concerning this matter. If it be so, our God whom we serve is able to deliver us from the furnace of the blazing fire; and He will deliver us out of your hand, O king. But even if He does not, let it be known to you, O king, that we are not going to serve your gods or worship the golden image that you have set up"—Daniel 3:13-18.

What determination to obey God no matter what the consequences! That they had no promise of deliverance is evident in the words, "Our God whom we serve is able to deliver us . . . But *even if He does not*, let it be known to you, O king, that we are not going to serve your gods or worship the golden image you have set up" (Daniel 3:17,18).

Small wonder the king was enraged! Such unyielding obedience to the God of Israel, whom Nebuchadnezzar did not know, infuriated him. This is usually the case. Earthly tyrants who would usurp God's authority are outraged when obedience to them is refused.

Fortunately for Shadrach, Meshach, and Abed-nego, God glorified Himself in one of the greatest miracles recorded in history. In bringing them through the fiery furnace unharmed, He honored their obedience to Himself, even though that obedience put them at odds with an earthly potentate.

"I Have Committed No Crime!"

Daniel, another God-fearing Hebrew, encountered a similar predicament under a new king. Because of his extraordinary spirit, Daniel distinguished himself among the all the governmental officials in the land. His promotion to prime minister angered a jealous group of his political contemporaries.

Those who unsuccessfully sought his demise finally realized, "We shall not find any ground of accusation against
this Daniel unless we find it against him with regard to the
law of his God" (Daniel 6:5).

These ruthless men knew that Daniel would be motivated
by a higher allegiance if it came to obeying God or obeying
the king. They devised a scheme that forced Daniel to make
that choice and thereby jeopardize his life.

The commissioners and officials persuaded the king to
establish an injunction and sign a document outlawing
prayer. How did Daniel respond when he knew that anyone who petitioned any god or man beside the king would
be cast into the lions' den?

> Now when Daniel knew that the document was
> signed, he entered his house (now in his roof
> chamber he had windows open toward Jerusalem);
> and he continued kneeling on his knees three
> times a day, praying and giving thanks before his
> God, as he had been doing previously.
>
> Then these men came by agreement and found
> Daniel making petition and supplication before his
> God. Then they approached and spoke before the
> king about the king's injunction, "Did you not sign
> an injunction that any man who makes a petition
> to any god or man besides you, O king, for thirty
> days, is to be cast into the lions' den?"
>
> The king answered and said, "The statement
> is true, according to the law of the Medes and
> Persians, which may not be revoked."
>
> Then they answered and spoke before the king,
> "Daniel, who is one of the exiles from Judah, pays
> no attention to you, O king, or to the injunction
> which you signed, but keeps making his petition
> three times a day"—Daniel 6:10-13.

An unwavering will to obey! Knowing the document had been signed, Daniel continued to worship as he had always done. Only a little compromise would have kept him out of trouble. He could have shut the window and prayed! But a little compromise was too much for Daniel. He paid no heed to the new injunction, but continued in his prior commitment to God.

As in the case of Daniel's three friends, God miraculously protected him. Daniel's testimony concerning his deliverance was this, "My God sent His angel and shut the lions' mouths, and they have not harmed me, inasmuch as I was found innocent before Him; and also toward you, O king, *I have committed no crime*" (Daniel 6:22, italics added).

Before God, Daniel was *absolutely innocent,* even though he disobeyed the king's decree. And, as Daniel stated, no *real* crime or injury had been committed against the king.

Who Told Them to Break the Law?

The New Testament begins almost immediately with an example of obeying God rather than man. After Jesus was born in Bethlehem, magi from the east arrived in Jerusalem to inquire about the Messiah. Having seen His star in the east, they had come to worship this newborn King of the Jews.

When Herod the king heard this announcement, he was very troubled. (See Matthew 2:1-3.) How did Herod respond to hearing that a new king had arrived on the scene?

> Then Herod secretly called the magi, and ascertained from them the time the star appeared. And he sent them to Bethlehem, and said, "Go and make careful search for the Child, and when you have found Him, report to me, that I too may come and worship Him"—Matthew 2:7,8.

They obeyed the king's charge to find the child. "And when they saw the star, they rejoiced exceedingly with great joy . . . and they fell down and worshiped Him; and opening their treasures they presented to Him gifts of gold and frankincense and myrrh" (Matthew 2:10,11). But their obedience to King Herod ended at that juncture.

> And having been warned by God in a dream not to return to Herod, they departed for their own country by another way—Matthew 2:12.

Imagine that—God telling them to break the law! Think of what would have happened if they had "obeyed the law."

Herod, determined to destroy the Child, "sent and slew all the male children who were in Bethlehem and in all its environs, from two years old and under" (Matthew 2:16). We grieve for those children and parents, but we also thank God that the magi refused to obey the king.

"We Must Obey God Rather than Men"

The preaching of the gospel by the apostles and other disciples in the early church was having a tremendous effect on its hearers; miracles were occurring, and thousands were believing in Jesus. This outraged the priests, so one evening they had the temple guard arrest the apostles and put them in jail for the night.

In the morning, a hearing was held and the Jewish leaders "commanded them not to speak or teach at all in the name of Jesus" (Acts 4:18), to which Peter and John gave the following reply:

> "Whether it is right in the sight of God to give heed to you rather than to God, you be the judge; for we cannot stop speaking what we have seen and heard"—Acts 4:19,20.

The confrontation, however, did not end there. The apostles defied the command given them, and obeyed the Lord's commission to preach the gospel. Their unyielding obedience to God further outraged the religious leaders. Besides that, the success the apostles were having filled the priests with jealousy. So once again, "they laid hands on the apostles, and put them in public jail" (Acts 5:18).

This jail visit was a short one, though, for God dispatched an angel to release the apostles and—imagine the gall of it— he commanded them to return to the temple and keep preaching! (See Acts 5:19-25.) When the captain and officers located them, they peacefully arrested them again.

> And when they had brought them, they stood them before the Council. And the high priest questioned them, saying, "We gave you strict orders not to continue teaching in this name, and behold, you have filled Jerusalem with your teaching, and intend to bring this man's blood upon us"—Acts 5:27,28.

Peter and the apostles then gave the most clear and concise definition of the principle in question:

> "We must obey God rather than men"—Acts 5:29.

Is There A Conflict?

One portion of Scripture specifically commands us to obey civil authority, and yet other passages show people *dis*obeying civil authority, under God's direction and with His blessing, approval, and protection. Either we obey Romans 13 or we don't, right? Is there a conflict?

I believe our Lord's own life provides us with the answer. Many times Jesus and His disciples were confronted by the Pharisees for supposedly breaking the Sabbath law.

And it came about that He was passing through the grainfields on the Sabbath, and His disciples began to make their way along while picking the heads of grain. And the Pharisees were saying to Him, "See here, why are they doing what is not lawful on the Sabbath?"—Mark 2:23,24.

They brought to the Pharisees him who was formerly blind. Now it was a Sabbath on the day when Jesus made the clay, and opened his eyes . . . Therefore some of the Pharisees were saying, "This man is not from God, because He does not keep the Sabbath"—John 9:13,14,16a.

And the scribes and Pharisees were watching Him closely, to see if He healed on the Sabbath, in order that they might find reason to accuse Him . . . And Jesus said to them, "I ask you, is it lawful on the Sabbath to do good, or to do harm, to save a life or to destroy it?" And after looking around at them all, He said to him, "Stretch out your hand!" And he did so; and his hand was restored. But they themselves were filled with rage, and discussed together what they might do to Jesus—Luke 6:7-11.

Two Reasons for Defiance

Our Lord's words, "Is it lawful . . . *to do good,* or to do harm, *to save a life,* or to destroy it?" hold the key to resolving any apparent conflict.

Numerous scriptural examples support two basic reasons to defy civil authority:

1. *Saving someone's life* (Hebrew midwives, Moses' parents, Rahab, and the magi);

2. *Remaining faithful to God* (three Hebrew children, Daniel, and the apostles).

When someone's life is at stake, we must obey God's injunction to "rescue those who are unjustly sentenced to death" (Proverbs 24:11, TLB).

The law of life supercedes all lower statutes that were established to protect life in the first place. If an earthly authority declares a law that contradicts this principle, it is of no consequence—even if that authority waves Romans 13:1-5 in our face!

Likewise, when God's people are asked to compromise their obedience to Him by order of a civil authority, God expects, no, *demands* that we remain faithful to Him.

We *must* obey God rather than men, whatever the consequences. Jesus said,

> "And do not fear those who kill the body, but are unable to kill the soul; but rather fear Him who is able to destroy both body and soul in hell"— Matthew 10:28.

Unconditional Obedience to Whom?

Christians who believe that we should never break the law *wrongly assume* that Romans 13 and 1 Peter 2 are the *only* passages in the Bible dealing with the believer's responsibility to civil authority. They are not! We must take the "whole counsel" of God on any doctrine.

For example, if a Bible teacher takes the verse, "You see that a man is justified by works, and not by faith alone" (James 2:24) and builds on just that passage, he will end up in error or possibly heresy. He must include other passages dealing with the believer's justification by faith.

In like manner, those claiming unconditional obedience to the government because of Paul's and Peter's writings err.

Romans 13 and 1 Peter 2 do *not* address the question of what believers should do when government abandons its God-given responsibility to punish the evil and reward the good, and begins to punish the good while rewarding and protecting the wicked.

That is tyranny. At those times, the biblical examples cited give abundant testimony that God *expects* His people to disobey the ungodly laws of men, and to remain faithful and obedient to Him.

For those who still aren't sure, I would point out that the man who penned Romans 13 also wrote four prison epistles! Both Paul and Peter were executed by the Roman authorities as lawbreakers.

Faith Not Rebellion

Four of the Old Testament examples who obeyed God rather than men are heralded as people of great faith in Hebrews 11.

> By faith Moses, when he was born, was hidden for three months by his parents, because they saw he was a beautiful child; and they were not afraid of the king's edict—Hebrews 11:23.

> By faith Rahab the harlot did not perish along with those who were disobedient, after she had welcomed the spies in peace—Hebrews 11:31.

Daniel and the three Hebrew children are alluded to in verses 33 and 34 where it says, "by faith [they] shut the mouths of lions, quenched the power of fire."

Please understand that the operative thought in this chapter is faith. The actions of these courageous men and women are not heralded as civil disobedience, but acts of faith and obedience before God. Breaking man's law was *incidental* to walking out their convictions. Faith and obedience to God were the dynamo of their lives, not defiance of civil authority.

We must understand this concept implicitly. God does *not* want us to despise authority or rebel against any little law we do not like. He expects us to be utterly faithful and obedient to Him, and if that obedience brings us into conflict with civil authority, then we *continue* to obey Him, no matter what men say or do.

In these situations, we should not be haughty in our defiance of unjust law. We should be adamant but not arrogant. Then God will be pleased and honored by our obedience to Him, no matter how our faith outrages earthly rulers.

Remember, when we face those critical decisions, we are not alone; we find ourselves in the company of the saints in the "Faith Hall of Fame," who undoubtedly cheer us on from their place in the great cloud of witnesses.

Are We Sinning By Default?

Some Christians have told me that we should only disobey man's law when we are commanded to participate in evil. Under careful scrutiny, however, this argument is not valid. Yes, when we are told to do something evil, we not only have the liberty, but an *obligation* to disobey man's law.

When the Hebrew midwives or Moses' parents were told to kill children, they said "No!" When the three Hebrew children were told to worship an idol, they refused. Christians tell me, "When the authorities tell me *I* have to get an abortion, I won't obey."

But how should God's people respond when they are told *not* to do something good? Daniel was commanded, "Don't pray!" Rahab was told, "Don't hide the spies!" The apostles were ordered, "Don't preach in the name of Jesus!" If they had obeyed those commands, they would have sinned.

Sin can take two forms: sins of *commission* and sins of *omission*. If Daniel, Rahab, and the apostles had failed to do their respective deeds, they would have been guilty of the sin of omission. James made this truth quite clear when he said, "Therefore, to one who knows the right thing to do, and does not do it, to him it is sin" (James 4:17).

Should a man or woman ever break the law? If that law requires they disobey God, yes. The question, however, should really be framed, "When man's law and God's law conflict, whom should we obey?"

Who deserves our ultimate allegiance? I again quote Peter for the most clear and concise answer to the question: *we must obey God rather than men!*

6
When Obedience is Required

Jeanne Robinson

Making the Choice and
Facing the Consequences

6

When Obedience is Required

Making the Choice and Facing the Consequences

"We must obey God rather than men" (Acts 5:29). This biblical truth has been lived out in the lives of millions of believers since the birth of Christianity. Church history is replete with valiant men and women who obeyed God rather than men, and risked their freedoms and lives to do so.

In this chapter we will focus on three major predicaments Christians have faced since the time of Christ: emperor worship in the first three centuries; American slavery; and the Jewish Holocaust. The bold and courageous examples of Christians during these times provides real life testimonies to the truths in discussion.

Making the Choice

The young church had barely learned to walk when it became necessary to put the Higher Laws principle into practice.

A law was decreed that all Roman citizens had to worship Caesar by offering incense to him as a god, thereby declaring their allegiance to the state. Jews, however, were exempt from this law and were permitted to continue to worship Yahweh only.

During the first three decades of the church's existence, many Christians were former Jews, and the local church had a close affiliation with the synagogue. Because of this association, Christians, including non-Jewish believers, were able to skirt the issue of emperor worship. By the time Nero came to the throne, however, the Jews no longer welcomed Christians in the synagogues.

Suddenly finding themselves under the displeasure of Rome, these believers were forced to make a choice: either obey God who said, "You shall have no other gods before Me" (Exodus 20:3) or obey Caesar who said, "Burn incense to me and bow before the graven image made in my likeness."

The choice to obey God was obviously the right one, but it cost literally thousands of believers their lives. Until the time of Constantine, Christians were the focus of ten major periods of persecution. Jerome stated that at the height of one persecution, any day in the year saw five thousand believers martyred for their faith.[1]

"Do Whatever You Please"

Polycarp, the well-known bishop of Smyrna, was martyred (approximately 161 A.D.) for his refusal to bow to Caesar. Here is a portion of that story, as recorded in John Foxe's classic work, *Foxe's Book of Martyrs:*

> The proconsul then urged him, saying, "Swear, and I will release thee;—reproach Christ."
> Polycarp answered, "Eighty and six years have I served him, and he never once wronged me; how then shall I blaspheme my King, Who hath saved me?"
> The proconsul again urged him, "Swear by the fortune of Caesar."

Polycarp replied, "Since you still vainly strive to make me swear by the fortune of Caesar, as you express it, affecting ignorance of my real character, hear me frankly declaring what I am—I am a Christian—and if you desire to learn the Christian doctrine, assign me a day, and you shall hear."

Hereupon the proconsul said, "I have wild beasts; and I will expose you to them unless you repent."

"Call for them," replied Polycarp; "for repentance with us is a wicked thing, if it is to be a change from the better to the worse, but a good thing if it is to be a change from evil to good."

"I will tame thee with fire," said the proconsul, "since you despise the wild beasts, unless you repent."

Then said Polycarp, "You threaten me with fire, which burns for an hour, and is soon extinguished; but the fire of the future judgment, and of eternal punishment reserved for the ungodly, you are ignorant of. But why do you delay? Do whatever you please."[2]

Upon this the proconsul had him bound and burned at the stake.

No Compromise

Over the course of nearly three centuries the persecutions saw thousands of Christians put to death by being burned at the stake or beheaded; they were crucified, fed to wild beasts, tortured, and whipped to death for their refusal to "obey the law."

Francis Schaeffer pointed out that from the Roman government's point of view, these Christians were not being put to death for their faith in Christ. They were killed for

their civil disobedience. Christians refused to swear allegiance to Caesar and to acknowledge him as Lord.

If they had simply compromised a little, believing in Jesus
and burning incense to Caesar, they could have saved their
lives. But they would not. Therefore to the Romans, they
were seditious, rebellious to the government, and guilty
of civil disobedience and treason. Multitudes of believers
confirmed the Higher Laws principle with their blood.

Slavery and Higher Laws

Excitement brews in the heart of any young person who
hears the true stories related to the Underground Railroad.
My heart actually beats harder as I read accounts
of breathtakingly close calls between slave-hunters and
fugitive slaves. And my heart breaks to read of those times
when the Underground Railroad was temporarily derailed,
and poor black men, women, and children were dragged
back to the evil cruelty of American slavery.

Before we take a brief look at this testimony of courage
and obedience to Higher Laws in church history, two truths
must be pointed out.

> 1. American slavery and biblical slavery have
> virtually nothing in common;
> 2. There was a great difference between being
> "anti-slavery" and being an "abolitionist."

Biblical slavery was primarily a means of relieving a load
of debt. For example, if I owed $100,000 and could not pay,
I could sell myself into service for a number of years to a
wealthy man who would pay my debt. In return, I would
labor in his fields, harvest his crops, water his livestock, and
take care of his house.

Rules were given to the Israelites on their treatment of
slaves. At the end of every seven years, slaves were to be

released. Also, slavery sometimes occurred as a result of an attacking nation being defeated and subjugated by Israel into forced labor. (See Deuteronomy 20:10-11.)

American slavery was far different. Slaves were obtained by kidnapping, or by bargaining with a greedy tribal king in Africa who wanted to decrease his population and increase his wealth. This was also kidnapping done *against the will* of the slave and for no crime or debt of his own. The Scripture specifically forbids kidnapping for the purpose of slavery, and calls for the death sentence of those who do it. (See Exodus 21:16.)

American slavery was instituted and continued for the greed and laziness of rich white men. There was no release of slaves after any number of years, and no (enforced) laws governing how slaves were treated. We must not in any way confuse American slavery with biblical slavery.

I Am Personally Opposed, But . . .

Secondly, during the time of legalized slavery in America, it is shocking to learn that there was a great difference between being anti-slavery and being an abolitionist. Someone who was *anti-slavery* could believe that slavery was morally wrong, but felt others should be able to own slaves if they wanted.

Or an anti-slavery person might believe in gradual, compensated emancipation, with the government buying and freeing slaves one state at a time. Still others thought all blacks should be colonized here in America or deported to another country and colonized there.

On the other hand, what the *abolitionists* wanted was simple and clear: the immediate, unconditional release of all slaves.

While many people in the north and south were philosophically against slavery, they were even *more* against abolitionism. The antagonism toward abolitionism is perhaps best expressed by the mother-in-law of Congressman Frank P. Blair, who lived during slavery times. "Of all things in the world I hate slavery the most—except abolitionism."

The word "abolitionist" carried a stigma with it. The attitude for many years in most of the north, and in most churches for that matter, was a lot like some people's stand against abortion today: "I'm personally opposed to slavery (or abortion), but I wouldn't want to impose my morality on others."

Who Cares?

The state of affairs concerning slavery before the war is shocking. Most people today have the idea that the north for years was demanding the end of slavery, while the south was demanding its continuance.

This is simply not true. While most in the south did demand the right to own slaves, most northern citizens did not really care. They certainly were not abolitionists.

Lincoln stated in a conversation with abolitionists during the first part of the war, "It appears to me that the great masses of this country care comparatively little about the negro, and are anxious only for military successes."

He was probably right. Thus there were northerners who were both anti-slavery and anti-abolition. Our nation was entangled in a sorry, schizophrenic state of affairs.

As the war progressed, however, abolition sentiment in the north grew extensively. The Civil War was not started primarily because of slavery, but slavery was crushed because of the Civil War.

Thank God, however, there were Christians (and some non-Christians) who took their anti-slavery conviction to its logical conclusion—that no man has a right to enslave another man against his will. Those brave people worked together in the now famous Underground Railroad.

A True Hero

Calvin Fairbank was just one of many abolitionists who risked imprisonment for his convictions. In 1844, Fairbank helped a black man, his wife, and their ten-year-old son escape from bondage in Kentucky. They were safely conducted to a depot in Ripley, Ohio, and continued on their journey to Canada.

When Fairbank returned to Kentucky to rescue the wife of a slave who had recently run away, this courageous abolitionist was recognized, seized, and arrested for helping the previously mentioned black family. He was found guilty under a law that stated:

> Any person found guilty of aiding a slave or slaves to escape from his, her or their master, masters, mistress, mistresses, beyond the limit of the State, shall be punished for each offense by an imprisonment of not less than two, nor more than twenty years.

Calvin Fairbank was found guilty and sentenced to fifteen years, but served only five years in prison because of a governor's pardon. In 1851, despite the hardship he had already endured, his compassion moved him to aid a female slave named Tamar who was cruelly oppressed in Kentucky. He succeeded in rescuing her and started her north on the Underground Railroad.

While in Indiana, Kentucky officials illegally seized him and dragged him back to Kentucky where he was tried again for helping slaves escape. He served almost the entire fifteen years before being pardoned again in 1864. Fairbank then married the fiance of his youth, who had faithfully waited twenty years for him. This courageous man paid a heavy price for his convictions, but four innocent human beings were given liberty through his actions.

Hundreds and thousands of Christians risked their freedom and lives to smuggle blacks to the northern states and Canada on the Underground Railroad. This period of American history is one of Christendom's greatest examples of sacrificial love and the need to obey God rather than men. The participants were normal everyday people who dared to do what was right, even if it was illegal. They were heroes in the true sense of the word and are worthy to be imitated today.

The Hiding Place

In Europe, 1937-1945 were the years of legalized mass murder. Every step of that holocaust was preceded by bona fide government decrees. An estimated thirteen million innocent people, six million of them Jews, died at the bloody hands of the Nazis.

Multitudes were seduced by Hitler's oratorical powers and followed him in his spirit of hatred and murder. But all were not deceived. Hundreds and maybe thousands in Germany, and later in the occupied countries, risked their lives by "breaking the law" and hiding Jews and other hunted humans from their slayers.

The most well-known figures of this illegal rescue work are Corrie Ten Boom and her family. Their experiences are chronicled in *The Hiding Place,* perhaps the most inspirational example ever written of obeying God rather than men.

From a human perspective, the story has unlikely heroes. An eighty-year-old man and his two never-married daughters, Corrie and Betsy, became the center for the underground in Harlem, Holland, after Germany defeated Dutch forces.

Our generation of Christians cannot appreciate the cost involved in disobeying Nazi law. Identifying with the resistance could literally cost someone his life. For this reason, many refused to get involved.

The following account taken from the book, *The Hiding Place,* is typical of the attitude the majority of Christians had toward helping to hide Jews. The Ten Booms had recently taken a young Jewish mother and her child into their home, but needed to move them quickly to another location for safety. When a clergyman friend of the Ten Booms came to their house, Corrie spoke to him privately.

> "Would you be willing to take a Jewish mother and her baby into your home? They will almost certainly be arrested otherwise."
> Color drained from the man's face. He took a step back from me. "Miss Ten Boom! I do hope you're not involved with any of this illegal concealment and undercover business. It's just not safe! Think of your father! And your sister—she's never been strong!"
> On impulse I told the pastor to wait and ran upstairs . . . I asked the mother's permission to borrow the infant . . . .
> Back in the dining room I pulled back the coverlet from the baby's face.
> There was a long silence. The man bent forward, his hand in spite of himself reaching for the tiny fist curled round the blanket. For a moment I saw compassion and fear struggle in his face. Then he straightened. "No. Definitely not. We could lose our lives for that Jewish child!"
> Unseen by either of us, Father had appeared in the doorway. "Give the child to me, Corrie," he said.
> Father held the baby close . . . At last he looked up at the pastor. "You say we could lose our lives for this child. I would consider that the greatest honor that could come to my family."[3]

As time went on, the flow of people and information through the Beje (the home and watch shop of the Ten Booms) grew dangerously large. Living under incredible tension, the Ten Booms never knew if they were being spied on or infiltrated. They did their best to keep the work secret, but it was simply not possible.

Were They Right or Wrong?

Depending on the way one chooses to view the Ten Boom family, they were either perpetually wrong for breaking the law, or perpetually right for obeying God's command to "rescue those unjustly sentenced to death" (Proverbs 24:11, TLB).

The work demanded that they steal food ration cards from government offices (without these cards people could not get food), falsify papers, and be prepared at any moment to lie. In fact, they had drills pretending Nazi raids, in which they were trained to say, "There are no Jews here. I don't know what you're talking about."

Before you judge them for lying, try to grasp the fearful reality they faced: tell the truth and send innocent people to certain death, or lie and protect the innocent from murderers while risking your own life. What would we have done? What would God have us do?

Let's make it personal. What if hostile soldiers broke into your home, intending to kill you, your spouse, your children, and your parents. If your family was hiding in the rafters, and the soldiers demanded, "Is anyone else here?" Would you turn your loved ones over, or say no? I believe Rahab's action and God's commendation of her actions in Hebrews 11 provide the answer.

To my amazement, I have had two people tell me that the Ten Booms were wrong, and that they should have told the truth! I hope that if I am ever being hunted unjustly, I'm not hiding in the rafters of those people's homes!

Facing the Consequences

On February 28, 1944, the nightmare the Ten Booms had prepared for finally came. Corrie was sick in bed with the flu when six Jews frantically scrambled through her room and passed through a small opening into an adjoining secret room built to hide refugees. Barely had they escaped when a Nazi officer burst into Corrie's room, demanding to know who she was. She and her sister Betsy were beaten as the Nazis pressed them to betray the Jews.

This marked the beginning of ten months of hell in prison and concentration camps for Corrie and Betsy. Their father died, alone and confused, in a hospital hallway shortly after the raid. The months of agony in concentration camps were as vicious as all you have ever heard.

Yet in such horrid circumstances, Corrie and Betsy reached out with the love and kindness of Christ to all around them, holding prayer meetings and Bible studies with the Bible they had miraculously and illegally smuggled in. Their testimony of courage, love, and forgiveness throughout these atrocities makes one blush with embarrassment at our own selfishness.

Betsy died in Ravensbruck toward the end of 1944, and Corrie was released on New Year's Eve. She made it back to Harlem and stayed there until the end of the war.

A Clerical "Error"

At the end of the war, Corrie began reaching out to war victims in Holland with the healing message of the gospel. Shortly thereafter, she moved to Germany to help rebuild the shattered lives of German people. From that time until two years before her death in 1985 (when she was debilitated by a stroke), she traveled the world, sharing the lessons of forgiveness and love she learned in those days of anguish at the hands of her tormentors.

In 1959, Corrie traveled with a group of people to revisit Ravensbruck, which is in East Germany. Only then she learned of the miracle. Her release was the result of a clerical "error." One week after she left, all women her age were taken to the gas chambers.

Blessed be God, who brought this dear woman out of the jaws of the lion and thereby preserved one of the greatest legacies of Christian love and courage in modern history. May God grant us a portion of that same spirit.

Have We Forgotten?

Finally, let's examine a season of history that is very dear to all Americans. That era has its historical high point in a document which begins, "When in the course of human events it becomes necessary for a nation of people to dissolve. . . ." The Declaration of Independence is a thunderous endorsement of Higher Laws.

You may be surprised to consider the Revolutionary War in the context of church history, but it is historically accurate. The Protestant clergy were the greatest force instigating and sustaining the revolution of the Thirteen Colonies' succession from England.

The Declaration of Independence—that sacred document to which Rev. Witherspoon affixed his name—was an act of outright treason against King George. When Witherspoon and scores of other clergy participated in or encouraged this rebellion, they were breaking the law. But these men incurred no guilt for their actions, for they were based squarely on the concept of Higher Law.

While we tend to remember the Revolutionary War in the framework of American history, it was also a critical point in church history. Christians who believe we should never "break the law" should scorn the memory of Witherspoon and George Washington and refuse to celebrate Independence Day!

In reality, every Christian in America believes in Higher Law. There may be times when Christians will have to defy civil authority in order to remain true to God.

The question is, where do we apply this principle in our contemporary world? Or even more precisely, "When should *I* disobey civil authority for conscience' sake before God?" Christians around the world, and yes, even in America are being faced with that question today.

7

Who's Breaking the Law?

Jeanne Robinson

Civil Disobedience in Today's World

7

Who's Breaking the Law?

Civil Disobedience in Today's World

Now comes the challenging part: applying the Bible's teaching on obeying God rather than man to *our* lives.

Most of us don't have any problem with the saints in the Word of God who broke the law. God obviously expected them to obey Him, and He blessed them for it.

We wouldn't argue with the early Christians who defied Caesar, or the believers who hid fugitive slaves or Jews from their pursuers. While no verse commands, "Thou shalt hide Jews from Nazis," it is agreeable to us to apply Proverbs 24:11 to their circumstances.

In fact, it is rather romantic to picture the heroic deeds of our spiritual predecessors, saying *"Amen!"* to their bravery, because it does not involve *our* making choices, taking risks, running scared, praying for *our* safety, and risking *our* lives.

We may like to think that had we been alive in those times of crisis, we would have stood with the faithful. But would we have? When the Higher Laws principle strikes closer to home, we shy away from taking action. The cost seems too high, the risks too great.

In this chapter we will examine four contemporary examples of people who are living by the Higher Laws principle: Chinese Christians, Soviet Christians, Bible smugglers, and those involved in rescue missions for the unborn. In a few pages you will be challenged with the question, "Am *I* willing, *today,* to put the laws of God above the laws of man, as it relates to the abortion holocaust?"

Chinese Christians

Discussing the church in China in the framework of civil disobedience is difficult and almost unfair. The discussion should properly revolve around courage, faithfulness, suffering, and martyrdom.

From our comfortable, shallow, protected American Christianity, we truly cannot conceive of being taken to prison simply for having a Bible study in our home. We cannot imagine our wives being forced to have abortions because we already have our quota of one child.

Choices we never have to make, questions we never have to answer, and unjust laws we never have to confront fill the daily lives of Chinese Christians. Let's examine the implications of only three of the Chinese government's official "Eight Point Internal Policy on Religion."[1]

> Citizens above the age of eighteen have the freedom of religious belief. That is, believers and non-believers will not interfere with one another's business and will respect one another without any discrimation.

That means anyone evangelizing is breaking the law, which directly opposes our commission to "go into all the world and preach the gospel to all creation" (Mark 16:15).

> Adolescents under the age of eighteen shall not be instilled with religious faith. But if they want

to believe in God of their own will, that is an exception.

That means it's illegal for Christians to instill their children with faith in Christ even though God's Word commands parents to bring up their children "in the discipline and instruction of the Lord" (Ephesians 6:4).

> Anyone who acts against the above regulations will be re-educated. If the offense is serious, he shall be punished severely.

"Re-educating" might mean being sent for two years to a work camp. Severe punishment could include public beatings or imprisonment. Shocking as it is, this is the testimony of a Chinese believer, "As for pastors, each has served an average of seventeen years and three months in prison for his faith, much of it in solitary confinement."[2]

We must marvel at and applaud the faith and determination of our Chinese brethren who follow Christ at tremendous cost. Their lives, the miracles God performs in their midst, and the new converts won to the Lord in spite of the law testify to the correctness of their actions. We trust that no thinking Christian would fault them for putting obedience to God ahead of obedience to the Chinese government.

Suffering Soviet Believers

The suffering church in the Soviet Union is also confronted with the dilemma of bowing to the state, or bowing to God. Christians are arrested, beaten, fired from their jobs, robbed of their children, imprisoned, and slowly killed because of their obedience to the Bible, and hence, their "acts against the state." At this time, thousands of believers fill hundreds of work camps and concentration camps because they are considered enemies of the state.

Peter Deyneka, Jr., the director of the Slavik Gospel Association, states,

> Persecution in the Soviet Union is not just imprisonment. Every Christian there experiences psychological, economic, and educational pressure. One of the most fearful pressures which all Christian parents face is the possibility that their children will be taken away. Some children are taken away and put in atheistic orphanages because of stringent Christian teaching in their homes. Because of this, every Christian mother wonders every day if it will happen to her children. This psychological pressure is real. The Communists use these and other experiences to keep Christians on edge with nervous tension.[3]

Obey the Soviet state, cease teaching Christianity to their children, denounce Christ, or at least keep Him a secret, and they could get along fairly well under the atheistic regime. But obey God, live by His Word, confess Christ, and suffer as a lawbreaker.

One famous story is that of Private Ivan "Vanya" Vasilevich Moiseyev, about whom Myrna Grant wrote the book *Vanya*. He was a private in the Soviet army, who simply obeyed the Word of God in fulfilling his responsibility as a Christian.

Let's examine Hefley's synopsis of this bold young man.

> Vanya's crime had been praying and witnessing. His first punishment was to stand outside in the cold for five days without food. When he refused to be quiet about his faith, he was ordered to stand for twelve straight nights in subzero weather. He survived this.
>
> Determined to break him, his commanding officer, Colonel Malsin, tried interrogations,

beatings, and prison. He could not be broken. He was put on trial for attending un-registered religious meetings during recreation time, and for distributing literature containing falsehoods and slander against the Soviet Union. "I have one higher allegiance," he testified, "and that is to Jesus Christ. He has given me certain orders, and these I cannot disobey."[4]

For his allegiance to Christ, he was beaten repeatedly, and finally handed over to the KGB. They beat, burned, stabbed, and tortured him to death in a soundproof room.

Because of the international outcry against human rights violations in Russia, some restraint has been shown by the KGB and police. But Peter Deyneka, Jr. states that the restraint has come in areas frequented by tourists. The Soviets present a facade of humaneness while beatings and imprisonment are still frequent in more remote areas.

These conflicts are not unique to Russian believers. For Christians trapped in communist countries, Acts 5:29 is a way of life. God's Law is supreme.

Bible Smugglers

As you read this, perhaps a sense of compassion for our brothers, mixed with anger toward their tormentors, has filled your heart. I doubt that any Christians in the west could fault believers beyond the Iron and Bamboo Curtains for "breaking the law" in order to keep their allegiance to heaven.

Yet many Christians in the west have difficulty when other Christians take "illegal" action based on the Higher Laws principle, such as smuggling Bibles into communist countries.

Hans Kristian, founder of Europamission, began sending Bibles in the mail to Romanians who requested them.

Soon, however, the government found out the Bibles were coming in the mail and put an end to it. Then Hans was faced with the decision of getting Bibles to the Romanians and other Christians in communist countries by other means— including those outside the law. This is his testimony:

> We prayed, asking God to guide us, and we concluded, as the early Christians had before us, that we ought to obey God rather than men. This would be our rule of conduct in all things. Where we could do God's will without violating human laws, we would. But whenever a government, capitalist or communist, sought to impose laws that, if obeyed, would cause us to disobey our Lord's commands, our duty was clear, and so would be our consciences.[5]

Amazingly, the practice of smuggling Bibles often comes under the scorn and rebuke of some western Christians. "Romans 13 says you mustn't break the law!" That's easy for them to say. They have a Bible (or two, or ten) collecting dust on their shelves. They can't even *imagine* what it would be like to be without religious liberty!

Brother Andrew, author of *God's Smuggler,* gave this stinging, profound, and almost comical rebuke to those smug, non-thinking Christians:

> Those who still debate the morality of doing so-called illegal things will have to do a lot of explaining when it comes to Acts 5:29. It is not just a verse, it is a principle. The most illegal action which Jesus ever committed was done on Easter morning when He broke the official government seal and came out of the grave. Are there any believers who object to that grand act?[6]

We trust not. These men are true heroes of the faith. Leaders in valor, sacrifice, and love for God and His people. Men with the spirit of Daniel and the three Hebrew children who would rather risk death than bow to the ungodly decrees of men. And yet for their daring deeds they receive criticism from some parts of Christendom. God help us and open our eyes!

Confronting Godless Laws

Some western Christians have difficulty applying the Higher Laws principle, especially when it appears that the Christian is acting as the aggressor.

For example, if I am worshiping God in my house, and the police break in and arrest me, they look like the bad guy. Christians feel sympathy for me. But when I take it upon myself to smuggle Bibles into a country and thereby I *confront* their godless laws, I am seen as an aggressor, and often lose the sympathy of fellow Christians. "After all, he brought this trouble on himself!"

But is that really the case? Don't we have an obligation to do the will of God, no matter what it is? If obeying the Word of God makes me look like an aggressor, or a rebel, should I not obey?

If I know something to be right, like smuggling Bibles, and don't do it, isn't that sin? (See James 4:17.) When a brother is arrested for obeying God and bringing His Word to people, why is he met with shallow, unthinking remarks from Christians who should know better? Because he is no longer seen as an innocent victim but as an aggressor who challenged the law!

James said, "This is pure and undefiled religion in the sight of our God and Father, to visit orphans and widows in their distress, and to keep oneself unstained by the world" (James 1:27).

If it became illegal to protect the fatherless, would we be right in obeying man's law, or should we obey God's commands anyway? If it became illegal in America to share Bibles, would we comply? If it were a crime to love our neighbor as ourself, would we stop unsolicited deeds of kindness in the name of Jesus because the government said so?

Called To Intervene

If the sacrifice of newborn children to the god of Molech became legal, would we be wrong for intervening on behalf of the children? God's Word says, "Deliver those who are being taken away to death, and those who are staggering to slaughter, O hold them back" (Proverbs 24:11).

"Vindicate the weak and fatherless; do justice to the afflicted and destitute. Rescue the weak and needy; deliver them out of the hand of the wicked" (Psalm 82:3,4).

Obedience to these commands means we would have to physically intervene on behalf of the children about to be sacrificed. We would then look like the aggressors. But wouldn't we still have an obligation and a mandate to save them regardless of what we looked like?

Isn't this similar to what the Ten Boom family faced? They were not being asked to participate in killing Jews. They were being asked to shut up and sit idly by while the Nazis killed Jews. They were told to mind their own business, and to not interfere with the German government's right to murder innocent people.

God Hears Their Screams

Christians in America are facing this exact issue in regard to the abortion holocaust. One and one-half million children a year are murdered on the altar of convenience, pleasure, and "freedom of choice" while most Christians sit idly by and look the other way. Why don't we sense the same urgency that the Ten Booms felt in rescuing the innocent from slaughter?

Can God look the other way while these precious, innocent children are ripped apart by the abortionists' deftly
maneuvered instruments or burned alive in the womb by
a hypertonic salt solution? No! God watches them agonize,
struggle, and fight; He hears their silent screams; He watches
as they slowly go into shock and die at the hands of hired
killers.

God sees it all, and to Him abortion is no different
from sacrificing a child on an altar to Molech. Both are an
abomination to Him that kindles His wrath.

What if we say we are not aware of what's going on? Does
God hold us accountable if we claim ignorance about the
horrors of abortion? What does God's Word say?

> Rescue those being led away to death; hold back
> those staggering toward slaughter. If you say, "But
> we knew nothing about this," does not he who
> weighs the heart perceive it? Does not he who
> guards your life know it? Will he not repay each
> person according to what he has done?—Proverbs
> 24:11,12, NIV.

Indifference is no excuse. God knows our hearts and
judges us according to what we do or don't do.

We must intervene to save the lives of those being led away
to death! Thank God, a growing number of Christians in
America are determined to hold back the slaughter by
participating in actual "rescue missions."

Saying No to Murder

During a rescue mission, a group of believers obey God's
command to rescue the innocent, saying "No! We're not
going to let you kill innocent children." The rescuers peacefully but physically place themselves between the killer and
his intended victim. This is done in a number of ways.

They may enter the abortion procedure rooms before the patients arrive and lock themselves in. They may fill up the waiting room or they may come before the abortuary opens and block the door with their bodies, their cars, or special locks, so that no one can get in. It can be quite exciting and a little frightening.

Meanwhile, pro-life counselors inside or outside the abortuary can talk with the mothers who are scheduled to abort their babies. They can win their confidence and escort them to a pro-life pregnancy center or to a coffee shop to talk.

Sometimes it takes the police hours to remove the rescuers. No children will be killed during that time. Sometimes the abortuary will close for the whole day. This gives the counselors the desperately needed time to reach the mothers—time they would not have had any other way.

Sometimes a mother will arrive, see the commotion, go home, and totally change her mind about killing her baby. In any event, rescue missions win a stay of execution for the baby.

Values Higher Than the Law

Chuck Colson, writing for *Christianity Today,* told about Joan Andrews, who is at this time in prison for trying to save the lives of unborn children. In discussing the Christian's loyalties owed to God and government, Colson wrote, "When our dual allegiances are at odds, there can be no question which takes precedence. Christians must recognize a transcendent order that guides their actions, even when it stands in opposition to human law."

A few paragraphs later he stated,

> There are values higher than the law. One of them, certainly, is the value of life, the principal value law is intended to protect. In instances where it is threatened, the law must give way. A lake

marked "No Trespassing" is legally off limits under normal circumstances. But to save a drowning child, the law could justifiably be broken.[7]

A "rescue mission" at an abortion clinic meets the same criteria. The requirement to obey a just law (trespassing) is superceded by the possibility of saving a life. Rescuers are almost always arrested and charged with trespass or disorderly conduct—a small price to pay in an attempt to save someone's life.

Buying Time To Save A Life

The difficulty in rescue missions is that the intended victim is captive inside the mother. In the case of the Jews or runaway slaves, the victim himself could be seen, touched, and helped. In the case of the innocent, pre-born child, the mother must be reached and won.

Unfortunately, she is often a willing participant in her child's death. But not always. Many times a boyfriend or parents are pressuring the girl to abort her child. Sometimes a young woman feels trapped and does not know there are people willing to help her.

Almost all young women about to abort their children do not understand what is going to happen to them. Risks and complications of the various procedures are often glossed over or not even mentioned by abortion clinic personnel. Women don't realize that their chances of miscarriage and sterility increase drastically after having an abortion. They also encounter the immediate risks of infection, excessive bleeding, or perforation of the uterus, which may result in a hysterectomy.

Nurses must account for all the baby's body parts that are scraped from the uterus during the abortion. If a tiny hand or limb is not recovered from the womb, the patient can develop serious problems later. How can these same nurses inform women that the abortion itself is a quick, easy procedure? Surely they must continually deaden their consciences to the horrors they experience on a daily basis.

Abortion counselors give the impression that the life within the mother is not much more than an egg yoke. These young women would be surprised to know that their six-week-old baby has a heartbeat and can already feel pain. Not long after a woman suspects she might be pregnant, the child within her has already developed fingers and toes. These facts, however, are hidden from pregnant women.

On top of all this, the conscience God put in every human being is probably troubling the young woman, and possibly haunting her. In any event, while she may be a willing participant, this is usually because she has been pressured and/or deceived. She is certainly not eager to have her child killed and often secretly wishes that someone would talk her out of it.

When believers stage a rescue mission, they buy the pregnant woman time to change her mind. The sight of a group of people being arrested for *her* and *her baby* has a tremendous psychological effect on her. The rescuers have given her child value.

What's Stopping You?

Not everyone believes rescue missions are right. Why? Some Christians, especially those a little older, are against rescue missions because they appear similar to the sit-ins of the sixties by the civil rights activists, or the anti-war demonstrators of the Vietnam era. Still others consider rescue missions only as "civil disobedience," not grasping the life and death reality of abortion.

Yes, rescue missions are protests that make a statement to the press, the public, and the politicians. But far more importantly, rescues are a physical attempt to save the lives of innocent children about to be murdered.

Rescues are not merely civil disobedience, they are biblical obedience.

With many people the real issue concerning rescue missions is not obedience or disobedience at all—it is *fear.* Fear of what people will think of them. Fear of being arrested. Fear of being uncomfortable and placed in a vulnerable position. Fear stops most people from participating in a rescue.

Why have we, God's people, allowed this holocaust to go on for so long? Why have we given up and not resisted the godless, murderous laws of men? Why have we failed to obey the laws of God? Because we are afraid. God forgive us.

Dietrich Bonhoeffer, whom we discussed earlier for his stand against the godless Nazi regime during World War II, wrote about fear in *The Cost of Discipleship:*

> Three times Jesus encourages his disciples by saying, "Fear not.". . . [See Matthew 10:26-39.]
> Those who are still afraid of men have no fear of God, and those who have fear of God have ceased to be afraid of men . . . The power which men enjoy for a brief space on earth is not without the cognizance and the will of God. If we fall into the hands of men, and meet suffering and death from their violence, we are none the less certain that everything comes from God. The same God who sees no sparrow fall to the ground without his knowledge and will, allows nothing to happen, except it be good and profitable for his children and the cause for which they stand. We are in God's hands. Therefore, "Fear not."[8]

At the beginning of this chapter, I said you may have to ask yourself, "Am I willing *today* to put the laws of God above the laws of man?"

Are you willing with a group of your friends to say, "No! We are not going to let you kill babies. God's Word forbids it, and commands us to try and stop you," and then gather around an abortion mill door? Are you willing to risk arrest to try and save the life of an innocent child?

Christians have a tendency to fantasize about helping Corrie Ten Boom or the Underground Railroad. What makes us think we would have aided them, when it might have cost us years in prison or even death? Today you can save a life, and all it costs is maybe your reputation, a small fine, or a few hours or days in jail.

Can Man Legislate God?

For any who still might wonder if rescue missions are a valid application of the Higher Laws principle, let's ask some basic questions.

Are we endowed by our Creator or by the state with the right to life?

Does *anyone* have the right to kill an innocent, defenseless baby?

Is God's command, "Thou shall not kill" eradicated by a Supreme Court ruling?

Is our obligation to obey the commands "love thy neighbor as thyself" and "rescue those unjustly sentenced to death" nullified because of *Roe vs. Wade?*

Let's use our imaginations to make the point. Picture with me, if you will, a group of believers who are gathered in a church in 1963 before abortion was legalized. To their surprise and amazement, an angel appears in the room.

The frightened, excited crowd listens as the angel declares, "Babies are about to be brutally murdered. A man is about to start killing them on Broad Street. God sent me to lead you in a rescue mission on behalf of those children. Take heart and follow me!" The crowd of believers follows obediently yet timidly to the abortion mill, which has a big "No Trespassing" sign on the door.

The angel and the people, knowing that a murder is about to occur, properly ignore the sign, march in, and find the abortionist and two frightened young women. One of the believers calls the police. They arrive in moments, hear the claims of the rescuers, and question the man and the women. In the trash can, the police discover the remains of two babies who were killed the night before by the same abortionist.

The police arrest the killer and congratulate the rescuers for a job well done. The mothers find help in their crisis, the babies are saved from certain death, the press writes a front-page story, and the believers become heroes in the community.

Ten Years Later

Now picture the same angel coming to the same group of people on January 23, 1973, the day after *Roe vs. Wade* legalized abortion. Imagine the angel explaining that children and mothers are in jeopardy, a murderer is about to start killing, and they should follow the angel once again.

One Christian sheepishly raises his hand and says, "Uhum, mister angel, perhaps you haven't heard. Yesterday the Supreme Court legalized abortion in America."

Stunned, the angel stops dead in his tracks and wheels around with a look of horror on his face. "What!" he exclaims. "Are you sure?" Several in the room confirm it with an oath. The angel, bewildered and confused, slowly sinks into a chair.

"I . . . I . . . don't know what to do," he stammers. "I'd better check with the front desk." He pulls out his angelic intercom, flips open the lid, and says, "Hello, hello, do you read me? This is Gabriel! Come in, I have a crisis on my hands!"

"Hello, Gabriel. This is the front desk. What's wrong?" a voice calmly asks.

"You'll never believe it. I came to lead a group of people in America on a rescue mission for babies about to be killed by an abortionist and I . . . I . . . I found out . . ." Gabriel starts to cry.

"What is it, Gabriel?" the excited voice asks. "What happened?"

"Well, you'll never believe it," he says, wiping his eyes. "Yesterday the Supreme Court legalized murdering babies and . . ."

"What? Are you sure?" the voice demands.

"Yes, I'm sure," he sullenly replies. "God's people here are positive of it."

"Hang on one minute, Gabriel." Some static fills the line. The group of believers look around at each other, anxiously wondering what will happen next.

The front desk comes through, "Gabriel, Gabriel, are you there?"

"Yes."

"Well, I checked into it, and you're absolutely right."

"I know I'm right!" Gabriel says. "But what do I do? Ask God what I should do!"

More static and a long pause. The believers glance back and forth at each other. Would they rescue the children as they did a few years ago, or would they scrap the mission?

"Gabriel, Gabriel, are you there?"

"Yes."

"He says you'd better not go."

"Are you sure?" Gabriel interrups. "Ask Him about Psalm 82:3,4 and James 1:27."

"Yeah, good point," agrees the front desk. Another long pause while Gabriel nervously adjusts his wings. After what seems like an eternity, the front desk comes back.

"Gabriel?"

"I'm here."

"God says you had better put Psalm 82:3,4 and James 1:27 on hold right now. The same goes for Proverbs 24:11, Leviticus 20:1-5, and any other place you find the command to rescue the innocent. He says they're not valid or binding commands anymore. You know, 'Render unto Caesar what is Caesar's' and all that.

"But He does want you to write a letter to the Supreme Court for Him expressing His moral outrage. Tell them He'll honor the new law as long as it's in effect, and He'll command His people to do the same. That's all. Come home. Over and out."

As Gabriel says goodbye and flys away, the bewildered believers are confused and relieved at the same time. They don't like child killing, and they want to save the babies; but they certainly don't want to confront the law and rock the boat.

"When the law is changed, then we'll be glad to rescue innocent babies from the hands of abortionists," one of them said. "In the meantime, we'd better get on with our meeting. Now, what color should we choose for the new pew covers?"

Has God revoked His commands? Are we living in a "period of grace" in which God's Word doesn't apply to abortion since man has legalized child killing? If Christians are exempt, then we need not trouble ourselves with rescuing the innocent.

But if God's Word still applies in America today, and if His commands are still in effect, why, then, are so many Christians thinking and acting as if God has made a new decree—and murdering children is now fine with Him?

8
Their Blood Cries Out

Jeanne Robinson

Who Bears the Guilt for
Abortion in America?

8

Their Blood Cries Out

Who Bears the Guilt for Abortion in America?

America is quickly becoming a guilt-free society. Children shift the blame onto parents, environment, or economic status for their problems in life. Parents blame schools, teachers, and peer pressure for the rebellion and defiance in their children.

We've attached "no fault" to words like insurance and divorce. Television commercials and magazine ads promote diet desserts that allow us to enjoy the taste without the guilt.

One of the biggest stumbling blocks to dealing with guilt is a refusal to use biblical terminology. Even Christians who fall prey to "problems" usually find no deliverance until they confess their sins and repent.

"Alcoholism" is now classified as a disease, making it more acceptable than drunkenness; "living together" is no more than a euphemism for immorality; and homosexuality, now an "alternative lifestyle," no longer carries the reproach and shame that once was associated with it.

The contrast becomes even more glaring in light of more serious issues. Infanticide sounds like another sterile, medical procedure. Euthanasia or "mercy killing" sounds like a humane option for a feeble, aging parent. After all, we can't call it murder, can we?

Is abortion any different? Have we emasculated that bloody act to just another medical procedure, no different than removing a mass of unwanted tissue? Do we really believe that an unborn child is no different than infected tonsils, an inflamed appendix, or an unwanted cyst?

Facts You May Not Know

A child killed by abortion is not a child at all, some argue, but merely a "blob of cells," "uterine contents," a *potential* person at best. Medical research, however, has shown that a unique human life begins at conception. Adding nutrients, oxygen, and time will only foster the growth and refinement of systems that originate at conception and mature in adulthood.

Before a woman even suspects that she may be pregnant, tremendous development has already occurred within her womb. At *three weeks,* her child's heart begins to beat. The backbone, spinal column, and nervous system begin to form. Tiny buds for arms and legs also appear during that *first month* of development.

Unmistakable facial features, including the ears, nose, lips, and tongue are formed during the *second month.* Brain waves can be detected, recorded, and read at approximately forty days. Cartilage begins to change to true bone, and muscle systems begin to develop in this miniature infant who now measures one inch in length. This tiny person begins to move imperceptibly within his mother, responds to touch, and feels pain.

By the *third month,* the child doubles in size and features are increasingly defined. Fingers and toes are quickly formed, complete with fingerprints—the marks that give a person a separate legal identity. Sexual differentiation is clear, and the infant already contains primitive egg or sperm cells.

During the *fourth month* rapid growth takes place. The infant is now eight to ten inches in length and may weigh over eight ounces. Facial expressions similar to the parents and grandparents can be seen. Eyebrows and eyelashes appear, along with fine hair on the infant's head. All the physiological systems necessary for life have long since been functioning.

When a woman enters a clinic that advertises "Abortions up to twenty-four weeks," she is not ridding herself of a blob of tissue, or something that looks like an egg yolk. She is destroying a six-month old unborn baby that looks very human and may already resemble her and the child's father!

When Is a Baby Not a Baby?

What do the Scriptures teach about children in the womb? Are they fully human, a total "person," or are they something less?

> And they were bringing even their *babies* to Him so that He might touch them, but when the disciples saw it, they began rebuking them— Luke 18:15, italics added.

The Greek word used for the *babies* Jesus touched is *brephos*. The same Greek word was also used for John the Baptist who was yet in his mother's womb.

> And it came about that when Elizabeth heard Mary's greeting, the *baby* leaped in her womb— Luke 1:41, italics added.

The significance? The Holy Spirit, who inspired the Word of God, used the *same word* to identify babies in the womb and those out of the womb. Why? Because from God's perspective—which happens to be the only true one—there is no difference between born and pre-born children. Both are fully human and made in His image.

This same truth is upheld in the Old Testament. Referring to the birth of Esau and Jacob, Genesis 25:22 says, "the children struggled within her [womb]." The word *children* is the Hebrew word *ben,* which is used interchangeably in the Old Testament to depict a person already born, including adults, or one yet in his mother's womb—there is no difference.

Probably the best known passage in the Bible concerning pre-born human life is Psalm 139.

> For Thou didst form my inward parts; Thou didst weave me in my mother's womb. I will give thanks to Thee, for I am fearfully and wonderfully made; wonderful are Thy works, and my soul knows it very well. My frame was not hidden from Thee, when I was made in secret, and skillfully wrought in the depths of the earth. Thine eyes have seen my unformed substance; and in Thy book they were all written, the days that were ordained for me, when as yet there was not one of them—Psalm 139:13-16.

Not only is a unique human being present in the womb, but God Himself is intimately involved in the developing process. To deliberately cut short a life in the womb, to destroy a child yet in the creative hand of God, is murder.

Murder or Manslaughter?

Some ministers, seeking to excuse abortion as less than murder, have misapplied the following verse to justify their argument.

> And if men struggle with each other and strike a woman with child so that she has a miscarriage,

yet there is not further injury, he shall surely be fined as the woman's husband may demand of him; and he shall pay as the judges decide— Exodus 21:22.

The greatest error in using this verse to downplay the hideous crime of aborting children is that the event mentioned in Exodus 21 refers to an *accident*. The men fighting were not deliberately seeking to harm the woman or her child. In abortion, a man is paid money to deliberately kill an innocent, defenseless human being. Deuteronomy 27:25 says, "Cursed is he who accepts a bribe to strike down an innocent person."

Secondly, the Hebrew structure of this passage is unclear to its exact meaning. Using the literal words found in the margin of the New American Standard Version, and omitting the italicized words that translators add to enforce meaning, the passage reads, "and men struggle with each other and strike a woman with child so that her children come out, yet there is no injury, he shall surely be fined as the woman's husband lays on him; and he shall pay by arbitration."

At the time of Christ, Jewish scholars believed this passage meant that the child was born alive, without injury; not that the child died. This would totally invalidate a claim that the Scriptures teach a child in-utero is less than human.

Even if this passage is speaking of a miscarriage in which the child dies, the child's death would have been an accident, or manslaughter. Manslaughter was (and is) far different than pre-meditated murder.

The Mosaic Law provided cities of refuge where a man-slayer could flee and live in safety from the victim's relative, the avenger of blood. (See Numbers 35:6, Joshua 20:2-6.) Therefore, even if this scripture is speaking of the accidental death of an in-utero child, which is unsure at best, the absence of severe punishment would be in keeping with the rest of the Law concerning manslaughter.

What is Bloodguiltiness?

Most sins committed by men against men can be made right, to one degree or another. For example, if someone steals my car, they can return it or buy me a new one. Even if the thief is never caught, and my car is not covered by insurance, all is not lost because *I still have my life.*

But if a man takes my life, if he *murders* me, no retribution can bring me back. No tears of sorrow can raise me from the dead. My wife will be a widow, my children fatherless, and I will be gone.

From heaven's viewpoint, unique *guilt* is also associated with murder. The Bible calls it "bloodguiltiness," or "the guilt of innocent blood," which is imputed by God to murderers and their accomplices.

When Cain slew Abel, God came to Cain and said, "What have you done? The voice of your brother's blood is crying to Me from the ground" (Genesis 4:10).

The Sanhedrin, fearing bloodguiltiness for Christ's death, complained to the apostles, saying, "[You] intend to bring this man's blood upon us" (Acts 5:28).

God warned His people in the book of Exodus, "Do not kill the innocent or the righteous, for I will not acquit the guilty" (Exodus 23:7).

Child Sacrifice: An Ancient Ritual?

If murder is the worst crime on earth, then one form of murder is the worst of the worst—child killing. Child killing or child sacrifice was the most grievous sin occurring in the land of Canaan before the conquest. Because the guilt of their abominable sins ascended before God, He planned to destroy the Canaanite nations at the hand of the Israelites. Moses said,

> When you enter the land which the Lord your God
> gives you, you shall not learn to imitate the

> detestable things of those nations. There shall not
> be found among you anyone who makes his son
> or his daughter pass through the fire. . . . For who-
> ever does these things is detestable to the Lord;
> and because of these detestable things the Lord
> your God will drive them out before you—
> Deuteronomy 18:9,10,12.

Yet amazingly, in spite of God's warnings, Judah's backsliding in the following years proved so dark that this is
exactly what they did. The following two passages reveal
God's heart for the children who met an untimely death on
the altars of idols:

> Moreover, you took your sons and daughters
> whom you had borne to Me, and you sacrificed
> them to idols to be devoured. Were your harlotries
> so small a matter? You slaughtered My children,
> and offered them up to idols by causing them to
> pass through the fire—Ezekiel 16:20,21.

> [They] have built the high places of Baal to burn
> their sons in the fire as burnt offerings to Baal, a
> thing which I never commanded or spoke of, *nor
> did it ever enter My mind*— Jeremiah 19:5, italics
> added.

Twenty-Five Million Murdered Children

Is child sacrifice an ancient ritual belonging to barbaric,
past civilizations? No! Child sacrifice is practiced every day
in hospitals, clinics, and doctors' offices all across America.
Because the tiny victims are concealed within the wombs
of their mothers, people never hear their silent screams and
rarely see their brutalized remains.

But you can be sure that the powers of darkness hear and see with pleasure. Satan receives the blood of these little ones as human sacrifice, and he is not going to give up this stronghold and demonic altar without a fight.

We must not be deceived, and we must not compromise. Abortion is nothing less than murdering babies. Because nearly five thousand children *per day* are being killed in America, our country is bearing the guilt of innocent blood.

Abortion was initially legalized in certain states in 1969. Most people don't realize that the *Roe vs. Wade* decision legalized abortion *up to the day of birth.* That means a women in her ninth month of pregnancy can abort her child without being held legally responsible. Since the first states made abortion legal in the late sixties, and since the Supreme Court ruling on January 22, 1973, legalized the killing in all fifty states, over *twenty-five million* children have been killed.

That's over 10 percent of America's population—more people than live in Nebraska, Iowa, North Dakota, South Dakota, Illinois, Colorado, and Ohio combined. The cry of their blood must ascend as a deafening chorus in the courts of heaven. An atrocity of this magnitude does not go unnoticed by the Almighty.

Abortion: A National Sin

Besides the guilt borne by those who shed blood, a bloodguiltiness is imputed to entire nations where innocent blood is shed *and unavenged.*

God solemnly warned the Israelites of this guilt, saying,

> "So you shall not pollute the land in which you
> are; for blood pollutes the land, and no expiation
> [or atonement] can be made for the land for the
> blood that is shed on it, except by the blood of
> him who shed it"—Numbers 35:33.

Under the Mosaic Law, in order for the nation to be free from bloodguiltiness, the murderers had to be killed.

The guilt for spilling innocent blood rested on *the whole nation*. The blood of the children cried out against everyone, even those who did not directly participate in child sacrifice. Why?

> You shall also say to the sons of Israel, "Any man from the sons of Israel or from the aliens sojourning in Israel, who gives any of his offspring to Molech, shall surely be put to death; the people of the land shall stone him with stones . . . If the people of the land, however, should ever disregard that man when he gives any of his offspring to Molech, so as not to put him to death, then I Myself will set My face against that man and against his family; and I will cut off from among their people both him and *all those who play the harlot after him,* by playing the harlot after Molech"—Leviticus 20:2,4,5, italics added.

Those who played the harlot with the murderer are those who knew he was sacrificing his children and did not deliberately try to stop him; or those who did not bring justice by stoning him to death after he murdered one of his children.

Thus, the whole Jewish nation came under the curse of bloodguiltiness. The blood of the children was crying out from the ground in the hearing of Almighty God. As we shall see in the next chapter, the only atonement for the land would be its destruction.

Who Bears the Guilt?

Can you see the similarities between child sacrifice in Israel and abortion in America? Like Israel, America is drenched in the blood of the children, and our guilt as a nation ascends before God continually.

Based on God's dealings with Israel, can we believe that unbelievers in America are the only ones who bear the guilt of abortion? What about the church?

"Not the church!" some Christians would exclaim. "We are not participating in this abominable crime." Oh, really? I know of many young women from Christian homes who have had their children aborted.

"Even so," some might think, "*I* am not participating in child killing. I haven't been involved in an abortion *at all*."

But does that make one free from guilt? What about Leviticus 20:2-5? Not only those who participate in child killing are guilty, *but those who know about it and do not stop it.*

So serious was the matter of bloodguiltiness that God made special provision for forgiveness when someone was found murdered in a field. The judges were to come and measure the distance from the slain man to all the surrounding villages. The elders from the closest village joined by the priests were to then take an unused heifer to a valley with a stream near the victim. There the elders were to break the heifer's neck, wash their hands over the heifer's body, and claim innocence in the murdered man's death, praying:

> "Our hands have not shed this blood, nor did our eyes see it. Forgive Thy people Israel whom Thou hast redeemed, O Lord, and do not place the guilt of innocent blood in the midst of Thy people Israel." And the bloodguiltiness shall be forgiven them—Deuteronomy 21:7,8.

For the Israelites to be forgiven, they had to be able to fulfill two conditions. First, they had to honestly pray, "Our hands did not shed this blood;" and second, "Our eyes did not see it." In other words, "We don't know who did this."

You and I cannot pray this prayer. We know who is killing the babies, therefore, we share in the guilt.

We Know Who's Doing the Killing

We know! They set up their nice little "offices" and run their polite little ads, "Abortions up to twenty-four weeks." We can see the abortionists get out of their fancy cars at the "clinics." We can watch young women and teenage girls go into the abortuaries pregnant and see them come out barren—leaving their dead children behind in garbage cans without even the decency of a proper burial.

We know who is doing the killing, and we know where. And yet, for the most part, we have done little or nothing to stop them. We don't even try to make their lives miserable for their trade in human flesh.

We have let them go on their way, killing child after child, degrading one mother after another, with little or no resistance. We've said in so many words, "I don't like what you're doing, but I don't care enough to try and stop you."

Hundreds and hundreds of abortion clinics around the country—and some close to churches, I might add—stand completely unchallenged by the Christian community. We know where the killings are taking place, yet we let them continue their bloody business. This is an offense before the God of heaven and earth. The church, by her *inactivity* for the children, shares in the guilt of their blood.

I am guilty, you are guilty, the whole church in America is guilty.

Where Have We Failed?

In response to child killing, God declared, "I will also set my face against that man . . . because he has given some of his offspring to Molech, so as to defile My sanctuary and to profane My holy name" (Leviticus 20:3).

When children were sacrificed, their death defiled God's sanctuary and profaned His name. Today, what is God's sanctuary or temple? His church! When children are killed by abortion, His people are defiled, and God's name is mocked.

In some ways, the church's guilt is as bad as that of the abortionist. Why? Because the church could have stopped this holocaust by now. We have the mandate, the manpower, and the money. But because we lack the backbone, and because of ignorant or cowardly leaders, the church has done almost nothing for the children.

The church follows the example of her leaders, and the example most evangelical pastors and church leaders have set is appalling. There are some—like Jerry Falwell, D. James Kennedy, Pat Robertson, James Dobson, Cardinal O'Connor and a few others, who have taken a public stand against abortion. But they are the exception, not the rule.

Some ministers have said, "Just pray and keep preaching the gospel, and the whole abortion problem will go away." That is complete folly. Fifteen years of that game plan has gotten us twenty-five million dead children, with the toll rising daily.

If just preaching the gospel was the answer, we should be the most righteous people on earth. The United States has access to more preaching than any other nation, yet we have become the moral cesspool of the world. Obviously, there is something very defective in that strategy.

The church leaders and, therefore, the entire church have tragically failed to contend with the bloodshed at hand, and we share in the guilt of this holocaust before God.

What Will It Take?

Now that we've acknowledged our guilt, where do we go from here? What does God require of His people? Let's look at a very fitting passage in the light of this holocaust:

> God takes His stand in His own congregation; He
> judges in the midst of the rulers. How long will

you judge unjustly, and show partiality to the wicked? Vindicate the weak and fatherless; do justice to the afflicted and destitute. Rescue the weak and needy; deliver them out of the hand of the wicked—Psalm 82:1-4.

What is this scripture saying? Notice that God is addressing *His* people (verse 1). If we are not defending the fatherless and rescuing the weak and needy from the hand of the wicked, we are siding with the killers! We are judging unjustly and showing partiality to the wicked.

We're saying to the abortion industry, "We don't like what you're doing, but we don't care enough to try and stop you." God will respond to us like He did to the Israelites of Isaiah's day:

"I cannot endure iniquity and the solemn assembly. I hate your new moon festivals and your appointed feasts, they have become a burden to Me. I am weary of bearing them. So when you spread your hands out in prayer, I will hide My eyes from you"—Isaiah 1:13-15a.

Why was God being so hard on them? After all, He instituted the festivals and feasts, along with the calling of certain assemblies. Why is He now rejecting the very duties He called for?

"Yes, even though you multiply prayers, I will not listen. Your hands are covered with blood. Wash yourselves, make yourselves clean; remove the evil of your deeds from My sight. Cease to do evil, learn to do good; seek justice, remove the ruthless; defend the orphan, plead for the widow"—Isaiah 1:15b-17.

When God's people neglect their social responsibilities, such as seeking justice, reproving the ruthless, defending the orphan, or pleading for the widow, their religious activities become a stench in the nostrils of God.

Today we have our elegant religious ceremonies, our special offerings, our seminars, our feasts (covered dish dinners), but we have not helped the helpless. We have not stood for the innocent.

Repentance and True Revival

Any "revival" in a given church or community that does not result in God's people repenting for allowing abortion to continue is false. *Unless the rights of the children and mothers are being defended, true revival has not occurred.*

Emotions may run high, church growth may even follow, but if the the broken heart of God for the dying babies is not being revealed in His people, then something is terribly wrong.

When Cain murdered Abel, God could not hold back His anger and His grief:

> The Lord said, "What have you done? Listen! Your brother's blood cries out to me from the ground. Now you are under a curse. . . .'—Genesis 4:10, NIV.

The blood of the innocent unborn is crying out. And what is at stake is terrifying.

Will America Survive?

Jeanne Robinson

Turning the Tide Before
It's Too late

9

Will America Survive?

Turning the Tide Before it's Too Late

Scripture clearly teaches that those guilty of shedding innocent blood will be punished.

When Noah and his family left the ark, God specifically warned him,

> "And surely I will require your lifeblood . . . from every man, from every man's brother I will require the life of man. Whoever sheds man's blood, by man his blood shall be shed, for in the image of God He made man"—Genesis 9:5,6.

Murder was the only sin that Noah was instructed to punish, and that by a death sentence. God required that justice or judgment should come on the killer *from another man.*

God's statute concerning murder was upheld under Mosaic Law:

> Or if he struck him with a wooden object in the hand, by which he may die, and as a result he died, he is a murderer; the murderer shall surely be put to death. The blood avenger himself shall put the

murderer to death; he shall put him to death when
he meets him—Numbers 35:18,19.

The killer reaped God's judgment when the next of kin
avenged the murdered man.

The apostle Paul, writing about the role civil officials play
in judgment, said that governmental rule is a "minister of
God, an avenger who brings wrath upon the one who practices evil" (Romans 13:4). God ordained that the first wave
of His judgment, or punishment, should come upon killers
and wicked men *through human agency*.

Will the Guilty Escape?

What if man failed in his duty to avenge the blood of the
innocent? As we saw in the last chapter, the guilt of innocent blood is then shared by those who know of the killing, yet bring no justice.

But beyond guilt, what of judgment? Will justice ever
come, or do the guilty escape retribution? Why do the
wicked prosper and seem to get away with their wickedness?

The simple truth is that wicked people, even murderers,
sometimes escape earthly justice. This fact could cause
us to question the sovereignty or justice of God, but the
Scriptures give us understanding and peace.

But the Lord abides forever; He has established His
throne for judgment, and He will judge the world
in righteousness; He will execute judgment for the
peoples with equity—Psalm 9:7,8.

While some ruthless criminals may slip through the cracks
of this world's justice, they will only fall into the courtroom
of heaven—a court where no deals are made, no crimes
excused, no details hidden, no lies told.

At heaven's judgment bar of pure justice *every* evil deed
will be exposed, and the guilty will be sentenced to

eternal punishment. Evil men may elude justice on earth, but "surely Thou dost set them in slippery places; Thou dost cast them down to destruction. How are they destroyed in a moment! They are utterly swept away by sudden terrors!" (Psalm 73:18,19).

That day of judgment will be more thorough, more *real,* and more terrifying than any judgment could ever be on earth. So let's be patient. God knows who the wicked are, and the day of judgment could be any day.

But what about justice here and now, especially against abortionists and their accomplices—those who willingly offer their children and those who know but do nothing to stop this holocaust? The Scriptures provide the answer, and give an example of the judgment that fell upon the perpetrators of murder.

Divine Retribution

In the Old Testament God commanded the Israelites not to sacrifice their children to idols. If anyone did, God said the people of the land were to judge and stone the killer. (See Leviticus 20:4,5.) Knowing that men would not always fulfill their responsibility to bring justice, God warned Israel that He would set His face against those who did not take action against the murderer.

The promise God made was this: "Either *you* deal with the child killer, or *I* will deal with him, *and* with those who let him commit this atrocity unpunished." Scripture records how God fulfilled that promise.

Manasseh, the most wicked king who ever reigned over Judah, led the nation into the abominable practice of child sacrifice, even offering his own son in the fire. The murder of children was so rampant that the Scriptures testify:

> Manasseh shed very much innocent blood until he had filled Jerusalem from one end to another—2 Kings 21:16.

Tragically, the Israelites had adopted the horrid practices of the surrounding nations.

> They . . . shed innocent blood, the blood of their sons and their daughters, whom they sacrificed to the idols of Canaan; and the land was polluted with the blood—Psalm 106:37,38.

Because child sacrifice was accepted in Israel (much like abortion is legal in America), and no punishment was brought on the killers, the fury of Almighty God raged. The blood of the children was crying to Him for vengeance—crying to Him to execute the judgment that man had failed to execute.

God therefore told Israel,

> "Because of the blood of your sons which you gave to idols . . . thus I shall judge you, like women who commit adultery or shed blood are judged; and I shall bring on you the blood of wrath and jealousy"—Ezekiel 16:36,38.

When Reform Comes Too Late

Soon after Manasseh's death, his grandson Josiah began to reign at the age of eight. Josiah was the most righteous king who had ever reigned over Judah. (See 2 Kings 23:25.) He had an incredible zeal. Josiah abolished most idolatry and child sacrifice for a season, reinstituted the Passover, and did more "top down" reform than any king in Judah's history. All his reforms, however, were not enough to avert the judgment of God.

The land had become polluted because of this massive bloodshed, and no atonement could be made to appease God's wrath. (See Numbers 35:33.) Scripture says,

However, the Lord did not turn from the fierce-
ness of His great wrath with which His anger
burned against Judah, because of the provocations
with which Manasseh had provoked Him. And the
Lord said, "I will remove Judah also from My sight,
as I have removed Israel. And I will cast off Jerusalem, this city which I have chosen, and the
temple of which I said, 'My name shall be there' "
—2 Kings 23:26,27.

The following passage records the wrath God poured out
against Judah to avenge the shedding of innocent blood.

And the Lord sent against him [King Jehoiakim]
bands of Chaldeans, bands of Arameans, bands of
Moabites, and bands of Ammonites. So He sent
them against Judah to destroy it, according to the
word of the Lord, which He had spoken through
His servants the prophets. Surely at the command
of the Lord it came upon Judah, to remove them
from His sight because of the sins of Manasseh,
according to all that he had done, and also for
the innocent blood which he shed, for he filled
Jerusalem with innocent blood; and the Lord
would not forgive—2 Kings 24:2-4, italics added.

The Entire Nation Suffers

The Lord would not forgive! The innocent blood
demanded judgment. Judah's cities were destroyed, the
temple leveled, men were killed, women raped, and a few
survivors were taken captive to Babylon.

We must remember that not only those who killed their
children suffered, but *the entire nation suffered.* Hebrew
people who would have never sacrificed their children died

by the sword, by famine, and by plague, just like those who did sacrifice their children. The wicked were dragged to captivity along with the righteous, such as Daniel, Shadrach, Meshach, and Abed-nego.

The parallels between Judah and America are undeniable. Child killing was "legal" then; child killing is "legal" now. Only a portion of the people killed their children then; only a portion of the people are killing their children now.

Because shedding innocent blood went unchecked, all Judah shared in the guilt; because abortion goes on unstopped, all of America shares in the guilt. All the people in Judah suffered to one degree or another under the judgment of God, and all the citizens in the United States will experience the judgment of God.

Will the Church Escape?

Can the body of Christ expect to escape God's judgment? Our apathy has allowed the slaughter of innocents to continue almost unchecked. Our silence has nodded approval to those in our land who kill children and exploit women. We have turned a blind eye toward this terrible injustice.

Before God judges America, He is going to judge us, for "it is time for judgment to begin with the household of God" (1 Peter 4:17). Because the church has allowed this slaughter of children to continue, we must face those blazing eyes from which nothing can be hidden. Because we have failed to protect the innocent, God is lifting His protection from us. We have bowed the knee to a godless system that protects murderers, so God is handing us over to that system.

Some Christians cannot imagine Christ sending severe judgment, especially on His people. They see Jesus as a nice, loving, non-threatening, mild-mannered Man holding a lamb in His arms. Unfortunately, our current concept of Jesus is more influenced by Renaissance paintings than it is by the Word of God!

Has Jesus Changed?

During His earthly ministry, Jesus spoke a severe word of judgment to those who would harm children. He said,

> "And whoever receives one such child in My name receives Me; but whoever causes one of these little ones who believe in Me to stumble, it is better for him that a heavy millstone be hung around his neck, and that he be drowned in the depth of the sea"—Matthew 18:5,6.

Can you believe Jesus actually talked about drowning someone?

But the Scriptures say, "In Him all the fullness of Deity dwells in bodily form" (Colossians 2:9); and He "is the image of the invisible God" (Colossians 1:15). Christ Himself said, "He who has seen Me has seen the Father" (John 14:9).

My point? The eternal Son of God was involved in the command to burn Jerusalem and raze the temple where *His name dwelt!* He sent the sword, famine, and plague on Judah. He willed judgment on His people. Has He changed? No! "Jesus Christ is the same yesterday and today and forever" (Hebrews 13:8, NIV).

In Revelation chapters two and three, Christ threatened judgment to six of the seven churches mentioned. For example, to the church at Pergamum He said,

> "Repent therefore; or else I am coming to you quickly, and I will make war against them with the sword of My mouth"—Revelation 2:16.

To the Laodicean Christians, He declared,

> "So because you are lukewarm, and neither hot nor cold, I will spit you out of My mouth"—Revelation 3:16.

Did any of those churches survive? Weren't they all spewed out eventually? Where the church once thrived in Northern Africa and the Middle East, Christianity has been almost snuffed out. Today Islam is the dominant religion, and the cradle of Christianity holds the child Mohammed!

Those churches that the Lord warned in the book of Revelation no longer exist. Let American Christians not be high-minded, but fearful, lest because of our own sin and unfaithfulness we, too, are slowly silenced.

Bowing to Strange Gods

The historical books of the Old Testament confirm the principle of God's judgment falling upon His backslidden people. The following verses capsulize a familiar, repeated scenario:

> Then the sons of Israel did evil in the sight of the Lord, and served the Baals, and they forsook the Lord, the God of their fathers . . . And the anger of the Lord burned against Israel, and He gave them into the hands of plunderers who plundered them; and He sold them into the hands of their enemies around them, so that they could no longer stand before their enemies—Judges 2:11,12,14.

Once under the subjugation of foreign nations, Israel usually cried out to the Lord in repentance. Even then, their change of heart was short-lived.

> Then the Lord raised up judges who delivered them from the hands of those who plundered them. And yet they did not listen to their judges, for they played the harlot after other gods and bowed themselves down to them. They turned aside quickly from the way in which their fathers

had walked in obeying the commandments of
the Lord; they did not do as their fathers—
Judges 2:16,17.

This happened again and again throughout Israel's
history. The Israelites would bow down to a strange god,
and God would hand them over to be oppressed. Sometimes
the oppression would come from the people whose god they
had worshiped.

The reason the church has not stood against abortion is
because Christians have bowed the knee to America's god—
the god of self. Humanism is the worship of man, or self-
worship. It makes life man-centered instead of God-centered.

We seek convenience, pleasure, and gratification. Isn't
the presence of this idol evident in some of the church's
popular teachings and emphases? Christians avoid discomfort, self-denial, and "rebuke the devil" when anything
difficult comes our way.

Crossless Christianity

The American church has by and large despised and
rejected the cross Jesus said *all* His followers must carry.
I am not speaking of the cross of Calvary where our sins
were atoned. We should love that cross with all our heart,
for without it we are lost.

I am speaking of the believers' cross. "If anyone wishes
to come after Me, let him deny himself, and take up his cross,
and follow Me" (Matthew 16:24). This is the cross we
despise. We are a selfish people.

The height of selfishness is to know someone is dying,
and to have it within our power to save them, but to choose
not to.

Martin Luther said,

If you see anyone condemned to death innocently
and you do not save him, although you know

ways and means to do so, you have killed him.
It will do you no good to plead that you did not
contribute to his death, for you have withheld
your love from him and have robbed him of the
service by which his life might have been saved.

The greatest indictment of selfishness in the American
church, and therefore our contempt for the cross, is that
we have *chosen* not to stop this holocaust against children.
When most of the excuses for inactivity are boiled down,
they have self-preservation, and hence self-worship at their
base.

What Is at Stake?

In the same way that Israel was handed over to their pagan
enemies, the church is being handed over to oppression from
the idol we have worshiped. I can just imagine God saying,
"Okay, you want to bow down to the god of self, and you
want to assimilate humanism into your worship? Well, *I'm
going to hand you over to those who live by the godless
system of humanism!"*
The recent outbreak of judicial and legislative persecution against the church is not the work of the devil; it is
God's judgment. Home schoolers are being hassled by school
districts; ministries are facing tax exempt status battles;
church-related schools are feeling the pinch of restrictive
legislation; common citizens are embroiled in freedom of
religion and freedom of speech battles; pastors are taken
to court for practicing church discipline; and homes for
children are being closed.
These conflicts are directly related to our failure to
protect innocent babies. We share in the guilt of this
holocaust, and we will be the first to share in the judgment.
While the cases of persecution I have mentioned are bad
enough, where will it stop? A Supreme Court that can

"legalize" child killing can legalize anything. The reasoning used to remove prayer and the Bible from *public* schools could be used to remove any religious expression, such as evangelism, from the *public* sidewalk and the *public* parks.

The notion of "the separation of church and state" will be used to silence political dissent from the pulpit. The Supreme Court (or some lower courts) could rule that devotedly Christian parents are unfit to raise their children in a "pluralistic" society. Or those who discipline their children according to loving, biblical standards could be found guilty of "child abuse."

Churches and/or church schools could be required to hire their quota of homosexual employees or face discrimination charges. In light of how far our nation has deteriorated already, these nightmares are right around the corner.

What is at stake for the church? Everything we hold sacred: our freedoms, our rights, our values, our Bibles, our families, and the very future we hope to deliver to our children.

Restoration or Annihilation?

The question is *not,* will America be judged? Judgment is inevitable because the blood of the children already killed must be avenged. Even if abortion were outlawed today, our nation will still pay for the blood of the past.

The real question is, will we be judged and then restored, or will we be wiped out, never to be restored? What form will God's judgment take? Will the judgment stop at AIDS and perhaps an economic collapse, drought, and famine; or will we become an ash heap beneath the fallout of Russian or Chinese missiles?

The answer lies in what action the church takes for the children. The fate of America is in the hand of the church. If we dare hold back those who are staggering to the slaughter, God may spare our nation. If we succumb to fear and apathy, our nation is doomed to destruction.

Although God's judgment against Judah was very severe, we can take heart that He let them survive as a nation. In fact, He promised them restoration.

> "They [Judah] shall be carried to Babylon, and they shall be there until the day I visit them," declares the Lord. "Then I will bring them back and restore them to this place"—Jeremiah 27:22.

> For thus says the Lord, "When seventy years have been completed for Babylon, I will visit you and fulfill My good word to you, to bring you back to this place. For I know the plans I have for you," declares the Lord, "plans for welfare and not for calamity to give you a future and a hope"—Jeremiah 29:10,11.

To the contrary, Assyria and Nineveh (her capital) experienced judgment unto annihilation.

> Woe to the bloody city, completely full of lies and pillage; her prey never departs. . . . [Therefore] your people are scattered on the mountains, and there is no one to regather them. There is no relief for your breakdown, your wound is incurable. All who hear about you will clap their hands over you, for on whom has not your evil passed continually?—Nahum 3:1,18,19.

To this very day the location of Nineveh is desolate.

The Time is Now

Will America survive or will we be a desolation and an astonishment to the nations of the world? Or worse, will

America be a society where Christian ethics and a Christian witness are effectively snuffed out? The answer lies with us.

Will we give God a *reason* to show mercy and restore us as a nation? Will we repent of our selfishness and boldly stand for the children, no matter what reproach we come under? Will we prepare the way of the Lord and make straight His paths?

The prophet Isaiah said,

> "And those from among you will rebuild the ancient ruins; you will raise up the age-old foundations; and you will be called the repairer of the breach, the restorer of the streets in which to dwell"—Isaiah 58:12.

Will the church provide God an avenue through which to bring restoration, blessing, and the reconstruction of our society? Will He find men and women to stand in the gap, men and women praying and working for righteousness, truth, and justice? Or in our spiritual stupor will we stagger to the edge of the precipice and plummet to our destruction?

The stakes are high, the cost is great, and the time is now. Only you and I, by the grace of God, can turn the tide.

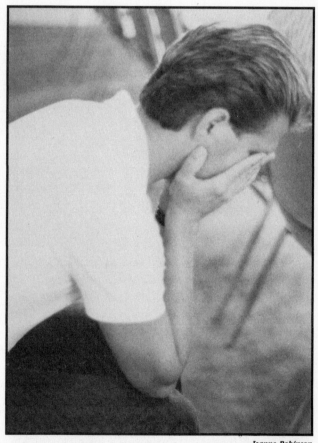

10

*A Remnant—
That's All We Need*

Jeanne Robinson

You Can Have a Part In
Changing America's Destiny

10

A Remnant—That's All We Need

You Can Have a Part In Changing America's Destiny

Deborah's day was a day like today. The hour was dark, and the situation appeared hopeless.

Israel had again entered into idolatry and assimilated the worship of the heathen around them. (See Judges chapters 4-5.) They chose new gods which kindled the anger of the Lord against them. God judged their backsliding by handing them over to Jabin, king of Canaan.

Sisera, the commander of Jabin's army, had nine hundred iron chariots, besides thousands of soldiers, and he cruelly oppressed the children of Israel for twenty years. The Israelites' crops were burned or stolen by Sisera and his troops. Common poor people were either killed or went into hiding. The following passage describes the situation in Israel during this oppression by the enemy:

"In the days of Shamgar the son of Anath,
In the days of Jael, the highways were deserted,
And travelers went by roundabout ways.
The peasantry ceased, they ceased in Israel,
Until I, Deborah, arose,
Until I arose, a mother in Israel.

New gods were chosen;
Then war was in the gates.
Not a shield or a spear was seen
Among forty thousand in Israel"—Judges 5:6-8.

Avoiding Confrontation

The enemy occupation was so severe, and the Jews so afraid, that they did not travel on the main highways. Why were the highways deserted in favor of roundabout, twisted ways? Because the Jews didn't want to find themselves face to face with the enemy!

Likewise today, most Christians want to avoid conflict and unpleasant situations at all costs. Most believers do not even want to *think* about unborn babies having their arms and legs ripped off, much less *do* something about it.

We retreat from conflict because we want to keep our dainty little world free from the uneasiness and tension that it brings. Because confrontation makes the "*me*-god" uncomfortable, we run from situations, words, people, or anything to do with conflict.

This dishonors God, for it is unlike Him. Jesus said,

"I did not come to bring peace, but a sword"—
Matthew 10:34.

The Lord endured one conflict after another during His earthly ministry, and He *promised* His disciples the same.

Because of our love of self, we desist from boldly acting or speaking out. We do not want to condemn or confront the world's sin as Jesus did because some people would not like us and others would despise and reject us.

Jesus told His disciples:

"If I had not come and spoken to them, they would not have sin, but now they have no excuse for their sin; . . . but now they have both seen and hated Me and My Father also"—John 15:22,24.

Don't Rock the Boat

I received a letter from a pastor who wrote *against* "civil disobedience." Part of his reasoning was that Christians need to maintain a good image in the eyes of the world!

This is a curse in the church, my friends. Jesus was called Beelzebub—the prince of demons—and He told us we should expect the same kind of treatment from the world. In fact, Jesus said that is one way we can identify with Him:

> "If the world hates you, you know that it has hated Me before it hated you. If you were of the world, the world would love its own; but because you are not of the world, but I chose you out of the world, therefore the world hates you"—John 15:18,19.

Why are we concerned about winning the approval of a world that crucified our Lord and hates all of His true disciples?

Some Christian leaders—professors and pastors alike—are teaching their people in word and deed *not* to get involved in controversy or "rock the boat." Their desire to avoid conflict and maintain a "respectable" image is often camouflaged beneath the banner of being "separate" or "loving." Seeking the approval of men and compromising to do so is an abomination to God.

Run for Your Church

As Christians, we would rather appear to have a good image and be "open-minded," than to be like Jesus—"despised and rejected by men, a man of sorrows, and familiar with suffering" (Isaiah 53:3, NIV). So we compromise a little, stay to ourselves, and keep from appearing too opinionated. The battle cry among many Christians is, "Run for your church! Avoid conflict at all costs!"

Under Sisera's oppression, the Israelites desired to avoid conflict so much that the "travelers went by roundabout [twisted] ways" (Judges 5:6). Why? Because during an enemy occupation, the enemy controls the highways and harrasses the travelers.

The church today has also taken to roundabout, twisted paths. We are running from the enemy and from conflict. We have abandoned the main highways of thought, education, the media, the arts, literature, the judicial system, and the political system to walk on our twisted but trouble-free paths. Therefore, we have become culturally irrelevant and ineffective, having little or no influence on our society.

Some believers think the "straight and narrow" means straight out of trouble and narrowly escaped!

Robbed of Courage

Like many of today's Christians, the Israelites of Deborah's day were afraid of confronting the enemy. And no wonder! They had lost their faith and trust in God. Judges 5:8 says, "Then new gods were chosen."

This tragic scenario is repeating itself in the church. The God of righteousness and holiness has been replaced by the god of tranquility, the god of prosperity, and the god of self-love. As a result, God's people have become apathetic and selfish. What happens, then, in a time of crisis? Do we end up like the Israelites, who when war came had no weapons to fight with?

> "Then war was in the gates. Not a sword or a shield was seen among forty thousand in Israel"— Judges 5:8.

How can that be? Why no sword and spear to defend? *Idolatry* had robbed the people of their courage to resist.

War is in our gates today! Demons and wicked men have been pushing back the church. What have leader and layperson alike been doing? Most of us are doing *nothing*. Not "a shield or spear" is seen among millions of Christians.

Two and a half decades ago when the Supreme Court banished prayer and Bible reading from public schools, did the church offer much resistance? What about pornography? Where have Christian leaders been while America's women and children have been sexually exploited by pornographic magazines and films? What have Christians been doing while our religious freedoms and civil rights have been slowly crushed before our eyes?

Most have been playing religious games, pampering and shielding themselves from all pain or discomfort. The church is already paying for this offense and will pay for it far more severely. But thank God for the *exceptions*—the courageous men and women who have taken a public and sometimes costly stand for righteousness.

Under Attack or On the Attack?

Some would argue that the church is not being beaten back—that the church *cannot* be beaten back. They quote the Lord's promise, "Upon this rock I will build My church; and the gates of Hades shall not overpower it" (Matthew 16:18), assuring themselves that the church will never lose ground.

This assurance proves false for two reasons: one, the true meaning of that promise; and two, church history.

Matthew 16:18 promises that the gates of hell will not prevail against us. What are the gates of hell protecting? The gates are for hell's defense—to hold back the forces of righteousness.

If the church is walking in faith, holiness, and obedience

to the whole Word of God (including social activism), Christians will be on the offensive, taking ground from the enemy and destroying the works of the devil. The gates of hell that would try to stop us will not prevail! This promise is *not* discussing the church coming *under* attack but being *on the attack!*

Scripture warns and history proves that when the church is *not* on the offensive—by walking in faith, holiness, and obedience—not only does she *not* take ground, she *loses* it.

Pillars of Jello

Tragically, many pastors today are only pillars of jello. They forever seek to upset no one, to step on no toes, to speak about nothing that is likely to offend. With an eye for the offering plate or having the biggest church in town, many seek to protect their own welfare and glory, rather than the welfare and glory of God's Kingdom. God forgive us!

Obedience to preaching the whole counsel of God—both blessings and cursings—is compromised for preaching the blessings only. Strong preaching on repentance, the believer's cross, and dying to self is abandoned and replaced with sermons on having a positive self-image so that everyone "feels good about themselves" and no one is driven away.

Preaching only a portion of the Word of God is bad enough, but the inactivity of many pastors is even worse. Their example of self-satisfied Christianity fosters an attitude among believers that keeps the church constantly in a position of weakness. No wonder we're losing the battle against the wickedness of our day. We have few Christian leaders willing to get their hands dirty and battle the filth being forced on us by this world.

The Height of Selfishness

The greatest indictment against the church for her self

worship is the virtually unchallenged slaughter of millions of innocent unborn children. Like the priest and the Levite, most of the church has "passed by on the other side" while over twenty-five million babies have been slaughtered in the "ditch" of America's abortion mills.

What would you think of me if I passed by a three-year-old girl, bleeding and dying in a ditch, and I did absolutely nothing to help her? What if I did not help her because I did not want to get involved; I did not "feel led"; I "wasn't called" to that type of ministry; or I was just too depressed that day?

You would say I was selfish, selfish, selfish! You would call me a disgrace to Christianity! You would be embarrassed that you knew me!

Isn't the analogy glaring? Millions of Christians, filled with a love of self, have these very preoccupations and use these very excuses while their neighbors—helpless little children—are being slaughtered. The height of selfishness is to know a person is dying yet do nothing to help them.

Repentance Brings Victory

Contrary to much teaching today, God does get angry. He even gets angry at His own people. We are not facing the burning wrath of eternal judgment, but an anger similar to that experienced by parents who have a continually disobedient child.

In God's anger against Israel, He often handed them over to be oppressed and ruled by their enemies—as He did in Deborah's day. Sometimes God would hand Israel over to the very people whose god they had served.

Oppression and persecution have their benefits. When God's people are under duress because of an oppressive enemy, they usually end up calling on God. But the first cries are generally for deliverance not for forgiveness of the sins that brought the oppression.

For years, Israel would stay in sin, and therefore stay under oppression, before they would repent of their sin. God did not send a deliverer until the people were *morally* ready.

Once He had their attention through suffering, God would send a prophet to tell them to repent. If they repented, they would have victory. If they did not repent, He would not cast off the oppressor.

As in Deborah's day, we are coming under some initial political and judicial attacks because of our idolatry. If we ever hope to regain our freedoms, if we ever hope to see abortion defeated, *we must repent.*

We need prophets—men and women whom God has raised up—to call the church to repentance for this atrocity against the children. Only when we, as leaders and followers alike, repent of our selfishness, our apathy, and our indifference will we be able to make the sacrifices necessary to win the war. Then God will fight with us.

Dealing with Idolatry

The church has *no chance* of defeating abortion, no chance of restoring our quickly disappearing liberties, no chance of bringing America back to moral sanity unless we repent of our idolatry and compromise. But if we repent, God can and will do wonders—even through a *remnant* of His people.

You remember the story of Gideon. God promised Gideon victory over the enemy—as He has promised us—but He told Gideon before he could fight the Midianite Army, he had to destroy the altar of Baal in his father's yard. (See Judges 6.) God gave him the hope and promise of victory first, but then commanded him to destroy the idol before He would help him overthrow Midian.

After Gideon destroyed the idol, his name was changed to Jerubbabel, "He who contends with Baal." God raised him up to deliver Israel from Midian, but his name was changed to "Contending with Baal." The lesson? He could not deliver Israel without contending with idolatry.

Likewise, we must deal with the idolatry in our midst before God will bring us deliverance. God is willing to avenge all disobedience, when our obedience is complete. (See 2 Corinthians 10:6.)

After calling upon God and hearing His command, Gideon and the Israelites repented. Only then did they have the assurance of victory. Notice these two important truths:

First, it is evident that not everyone in Israel repented.

Second, only a small minority of God's people actually entered the battle, but God gave them victory in spite of their limited numbers.

"For the Lord is not restrained to save by many or by few" (1 Samuel 14:6).

God Can Use a Remnant

These truths are critical in our hope for revival and reformation in America. The whole church may not repent of its inactivity, compromise, and idolatry. But if even a remnant will repent, seek the face of God, and prepare for battle, it would be enough to move the hand of God.

We should not expect the majority of the church to join the battle, nor should we be disappointed when they do not.

When Deborah and Barak rose up under the direction of God, only ten thousand were necessary for victory. Thousands upon thousands of Israelites sat on the sidelines as spectators. Deborah declared,

"Gilead remained across the Jordan; and why did Dan stay in ships? Asher sat at the seashore, and remained by its landings"—Judges 5:17.

The truth is, many will not fight, but that must not discourage us. Let us take heart. If God could use Gideon and three hundred men to route 134,000 Midianites, He can certainly use a remnant of His church to turn the tide in this nation.

Idolaters Turned Warriors

An incredible miracle happened when the people of Deborah's day repented. They became willing to fight. Before, they had been hiding and cowering in the mountains in fear, avoiding the highways and taking twisted paths. Now they were ready to die.

> Then survivors came down to the nobles; the people of the Lord came down to me as warriors. . . .
> And the princes of Issachar were with Deborah; as was Issachar, so was Barak; into the valley they rushed at his heels; among the divisions of Reuben there were great resolves of heart. . . . Zebulun was a people who despised their lives even to death, and Naphtali also, on the high places of the field—Judges 5:13,15,18.

Idolatry had robbed them of courage, but repentance produced in them a stout spirit, a willingness to die for God and His people.

Oh, the blessing of turning from idolatrous self-love! Only then can we become true warriors. Only when self-preservation is cast aside can we lay down our lives in battle.

Only those with warriors' hearts can turn this nation around. Warriors are disciplined, willing to sacrifice, and ready to die. They obey the orders of their commanding officer. God is looking for warriors in this day to fight in the war to end child killing.

What Will It Take?

While repentance was a key factor in the Israelite victory over their enemy, another point greatly contributed:

> "The leaders led in Israel ... the people volunteered"—Judges 5:2.

The leaders, who had been weak, began to lead the people into battle. The people, who had been glad to avoid conflict, volunteered to lay down their lives in battle. When God's people and God's leaders were *both* willing to fight, God undertook on their behalf.

The Israelites also had supernatural help. Verse 20 reads:

> "The stars fought from heaven, from their courses they fought against Sisera."

The "stars" speak of the angelic hosts fighting alongside God's people. When Israel repented and fought, God ordered the hosts of heaven to join the fight. And we know who won!

If we would see children and mothers saved, the church revived, America reformed, and severe judgment averted, we must have all these forces working in unison. God's *leaders* must lead the way in righteousness and reformation; the *people* must volunteer to fight and work for change; and the *angels,* the unseen forces of God, must fight alongside us.

We must have *all three.* If the people will fight but there is no strong leadership, they will fail. If the leaders will lead and the people won't volunteer, we will lose. If the leaders and the people go to battle alone, without the power of the Holy Spirit and God's angels, we will be defeated.

But if we have all three fighting together as the host of the Lord, I am convinced we can change the course of America's destiny.

What Our Nation Can Be

Before Deborah sang her glorious song of victory—and before we will sing ours—the people of God must see their sin and repent, then God will bring restoration to this nation.

If we repent, America can be turned. Righteousness could once again be honored and dominate the consensus. Wickedness would be called what it is—wickedness—instead of being flaunted and glorified.

We will defeat the abortion holocaust, restore religious and civil liberties to individuals, bring justice to our judicial system, see common decency return, and the godless, hedonistic, sexually perverted mindset of today pushed back into the closet—and hopefully back to hell where it came from.

Will we have a perfect nation? No. We are all imperfect people. Will we have a "Christian" nation? No. The Church is the only Christian nation. (See 1 Peter 2:9.)

What we *can* work for, believe for, and struggle for is a nation where once again the Judeo-Christian ethic is the foundation for our politics, our judicial system, and our public morality; a nation not floating in the uncertain sea of humanism, but a country whose unmoving bedrock is Higher Laws.

Commit yourself to make this vision a reality while we still have time. Please, for God's sake, for the sake of the babies and the mothers, and for our children's sake.

11
There's a War Going On

Jeanne Robinson

Finding Your Place
In the Battle

11

There's a War Going On

Finding Your Place in the Battle

America is racing toward God's judgment. The sex-related sins of pornography, the sexual exploitation of children, homosexuality, immorality, and adultery probably make us look like Sodom and Gomorrah before God.

Our public school systems have banned prayer, treated the Scriptures with contempt, and ridiculed strict moral teaching as old-fashioned and obsolete. Instead, children are gradually brainwashed with situational ethics and liberal, atheistic morals. Parental authority is undermined or ignored.

The media, theatre, television, movie, and entertainment industries perpetually glorify the philosophies and lifestyles that are destroying this nation.

Our judicial system is often a mockery of justice and stands in need of some drastic overhaul. Jails are filled with offenders who should only have to make restitution while more hardened and violent criminals are often paroled or placed on probation after serving a fraction of their sentences.

Our country is in desperate need of large-scale reformation. With so many issues raging, where should a Christian channel his efforts, time, and money? How can a believer discern which gap God is calling him to fill? Should our involvement be dictated by our interests, preferences, or what is convenient for us to do?

Our Highest Priority

In spite of how critical these different issues are, the paramount life or death battle before the church is to end the abortion holocaust against children.

If we righted every wrong, rectified every evil, solved every problem just mentioned, and yet did not end this slaughter of innocents, America and the church would still bear the guilt for their deaths. The blood of the children would still cry to God for vengeance. According to the promises, declarations, and warnings in God's Word, He would avenge their blood.

The number one social priority facing the church in America must be to end this slaughter of children. No other sin mentioned can match the level of shedding innocent blood. Halting this atrocity demands the immediate, concerted, and sacrificial effort of the church. The fate of America, and the future existence of the church, is bound up in the fate of the children.

If we successfully mobilize enough of God's people to end this holocaust, we will have the power and momentum to bring a major change in other critical areas of our culture. A resounding victory against abortion would start a domino effect that could go as far as the grace of God and hard work would take us! I'm not saying we should abandon those other critical fights; *absolutely not!* But I am saying we should *all* do something to end this war against children.

The First Step Toward Victory

Where do we fight? Where does *each person* lay his hand?

While it is every Christian's duty to do *something* for the children, we know that not everyone can be a full-time pro-life activist, any more than everyone can be a full-time missionary to Mexico. But we can *all* do something.

First, we need to repent for our apathy, indifference, and inactivity in defending the unborn. We have to acknowledge before God that *we* are part of the problem, and that we all share in the guilt of this innocent blood. We need to display the same spirit as these brave German Christians who actually fought against the Nazis for years:

> In 1945, the survivors of the German resistance met at Stuttgart with representatives from sister churches in other countries which had suffered mightily at the hands of the Nazis to proclaim a "confession of guilt." They implored God's forgiveness that they had not prayed more faithfully, believed more intensely, witnessed more courageously, and loved more devotedly. The Germans, as new leaders of the Evangelical Church in Germany, confessed their solidarity with the guilt of the German nation for crimes against humanity.[1]

Repentance is always the first step toward victory for the people of God.

Declaring War On Abortion

Next, we need to "declare war" on the child killing industry. In a time of war, a nation pulls together to defeat the enemy.

Some well-meaning believers might ask, "Is *every* Christian 'called' to the pro-life battle?" To that I would respond, "Is *every* Christian 'called' to love his neighbor as himself?"

Yes, everyone is called to do *something*. The war is everyone's business. The church is the "holy nation" (1 Peter 2:9) that must rise to protect these innocent children, rescue mothers from exploitation, and defeat the enemy of legalized abortion.

During war, the whole nation has certain responsibilities. Some are front-line soldiers, some are medics, others do recruiting, and some make ammunition. Everyone who works pays taxes to support the troops. There are diplomats and family members. Everyone prays.

The most critical need in the war against abortion is for *front-line soldiers* who are willing to place their bodies where the battle rages. Rescuers, who have been motivated by Higher Laws and a burning desire to save the children scheduled to die *today* are answering the call to the trenches in increasing number.

We need more men and women of conviction who will join in rescue missions and surround the places of death to prevent the killers from reaching their intended victims. Rescuers experience the greatest risk among the ranks of pro-lifers, but their courageous actions are the most practical way to intervene for the children scheduled to die *that day.* Participating in a rescue has the most effective long-range results toward making child killing illegal.

Backing Up the Troops

Right behind the rescuers we need *picketers and sidewalk counselors* present at the enemy's stronghold, pleading for the lives of the children. The greatest chance of rescuing children is when these two forces work together.

While the rescuers are in the clinic or surrounding the door on the outside, no children will be killed. Meanwhile, sidewalk counselors have ample time to talk with the mothers, win their confidence, and persuade them to go to a pro-life pregnancy center.

Sidewalk counseling without a rescue mission has resulted in many children being saved, but some mothers cannot be reached by sidewalk counseling alone. They can only be reached with the time bought by a rescue mission.

Recruiters are critical in every war effort. I compare recruiters to those who educate churches, schools, and civic groups on the horrible truth about abortion. Through powerful films, slides, and literature, recruiters can share God's commands to defend the innocent. Recruiters enlist new troops in the battle for the children and are a vital part of the effort to end this bloodshed.

Ammunition is needed to assault an enemy. Organizations that print pamphlets and manufacture cassettes, films, and videos are the suppliers of ammunition. Unfortunately, one of the most powerful pro-life weapons is a picture of an aborted baby. These graphic pictures and films speak louder than all the lying rhetoric of the pro-abortion movement combined. Our nation must face the nameless, innocent victims of this holocaust.

Non-Combat Personnel

I liken *medics* to those who respond with acts of mercy. When a woman considering abortion decides to give life to her baby, she may need help. Some young women come from horrible home situations and need a place to live while they are pregnant. Others need baby clothes and furniture, someone to take them to the doctor, financial help, or just a friend.

Still other women will consider placing their child for adoption. We must be sure to take them to a Christian adoption agency. Then the baby will go to a Bible-believing family. Government agencies obviously cannot make that commitment.

Family members are those who encourage the troops and stay in constant contact with the government, insisting on a speedy end to the war. Lobbying politicians by letter, phone, and in person is an important way to exert pressure that the law be changed. Also, writing letters and making phone calls to the judge and district attorney when Christians are being tried for rescue missions put pressure on them to be lenient if the defendants are found guilty.

Those who work at *crisis pregnancy centers* are a critical asset in this lifesaving work. Many women contemplating abortion go to crisis pregnancy centers for free pregnancy testing and counseling.

Eighty to ninety percent of those women considering abortion, and about half of those *determined* to have their child killed change their minds and whole-heartedly choose life for their babies. These pregnancy centers have resulted in multiplied thousands of children and their mothers being rescued from the death and horror of abortion.

Every war must be underwritten financially. In times of national conflict, those not involved directly in the fighting pay taxes to support the troops. This is a critical element in the war for children's lives. If victory is to be had, finances will be needed. *Those who support pro-life groups financially* provide a tremendous help in this lifesaving work and share in the reward for saving lives.

Finally, the whole nation needs to pray during a war. *Intercessors and prayer warriors* can stand in the gap and tear down the enemy's spiritual strongholds. We must beseech God for His blessing in this fight.

As King David said,

> Oh give us help against the adversary, for deliverance by man is in vain. Through God we shall do valiantly; and it is He who will tread down our adversaries—Psalm 108:12,13.

Finding Your Place in the War

Can you see that there is a place for everyone in this war? Can you grasp that *everyone* must do *something?*

Where would rescue missions be without the support of picketers and sidewalk counselors to reach the mothers? What good would letter-writers and lobbyists do without picketers and rescuers keeping abortion a "hot issue"?

Where would the operators of crisis pregnancy centers be without "medics" to help the mothers who choose life? Why have recruiters if they have nothing to recruit soldiers for? What would full-time activists do without the financial support of the faithful? Where would any of us be without ammunition? How could we even hope to win without the prayers of God's people?

The church must work in unison, and we must *all* do our part if we hope to save children now and succeed in securing justice for the children in the future. We should, therefore, be humble, not haughty, in our assessment of whatever work we do and thankful for whatever others are doing.

All the while, we should encourage each other to sacrifice *more* for the *children's and the mother's sake,* until we win this war.

Needed: Front-Line Soldiers

In this war against abortion, there are several things we can all do. We should select pro-life doctors, patronize pro-life hospitals, picket at local abortion clinics, write our legislators, and get involved with crisis pregnancy centers. But there is *no chance* of victory unless a sufficient number of believers confront the enemy on the front lines.

A nation could have praying people, ammunition, recruiters, concerned family members, medics, and counter intelligence, but without foot soldiers to take enemy ground, victory would be impossible.

Likewise, the battle for children's lives desperately needs front-line foot soldiers. In order to save children and mothers now and turn the tide of abortion, there must be a massive increase in the number of Christians repeatedly participating in rescue missions.

Millions of rescuers may not be required to turn the tide; perhaps a remnant of thousands could do it. But unless a ground swell of participation occurs, victory will not be possible.

It's Not Too Late

God will not strongly aid the church in overcoming abortion while the church is bowing the knee to Caesar, saying, "We will follow your commands. You can legalize killing, and we won't interfere."

Hosea 5:11 reads,

> Ephraim is oppressed, crushed in judgment, because he was determined to follow man's command.

As long as God's people are determined to follow man's laws above the commands of God, and as long as Christians honor government above God, we *cannot* win—for this is idolatry. If the church doesn't change their allegiance, we will be oppressed in the political system and crushed in the judicial system.

Can you imagine how different America would be, if the church had risen up when *Roe vs. Wade* became law? What if Christian leaders had said, "You expect us to be accomplices to this murder by sitting idly by while you kill children? You expect us to honor murderous laws of man above God's commands? You must be crazy!"

What if pastors had said to their congregations, "Come on, let's go!" and surrounded abortion mills, refusing to allow the wicked to kill children? This holocaust would have ground to a halt almost immediately.

But as history reveals, 99% of the church have honored

the laws of man above the laws of God. Because of our inbred sense of "obeying the law" mixed with fear of confrontation, we have tried to take the easy way out, the way of least resistance and least sacrifice, and have *miserably failed.*

More than twenty-five million children are dead, and we are as far away from a constitutional amendment to outlaw child killing as we have ever been. How many more must die before our congressmen and senators will take action? There has never even been a debate on the House floor concerning a constitutional amendment to end the killing.

In spite of our sins of omission, it is not too late. If we will repent of our inactivity and confront this evil in God's strength, we can win. In order to be victorious, a portion of the church must go down to these places of death as frontline soldiers to protect children and mothers and challenge the entire legal system that allows and endorses murder. That would mark the beginning of the end of the abortion holocaust.

A Reason for Restoration

I believe God is looking for a reason *not* to judge America into oblivion, but rather to chasten her and restore her. We must give Him a reason to show mercy.

If we answer the call of God to stand in the gap by repentance, prayer, and action, I believe America will be restored. If we do not, God only knows what terrors the future holds for us and our children.

Are you unnerved at the thought of Christians repenting of their apathy, defending children and mothers, and causing a social upheaval or a peaceful uprising? So am I! But I am more afraid of what will happen if we do *not* act. Remember, courage is not the absence of fear, but a will to fight *in spite of our fears.* Every time I am involved in a rescue, I am scared.

The children are crying for deliverance. God is looking for people to stand in the gap. Whatever He asks you to do, do it, and leave the results with Him. Risks must be taken and sacrifices made. But if we "prepare the way," then when God does visit America it can result in revival and reformation, not judgment and annihilation.

Remember, the fate of America is bound up in the innocent blood of the children. What *we* do for them will determine what God does in the years to come.

12
Called to the Front Lines

Lyn Cryderman

How We Can Confront the Enemy
And Win the War

12

Called to the Front Lines

How We Can Confront the Enemy And Win the War

We're all familiar with the Battle of Jericho. (See Joshua 6.) God promised that He would fight for the Israelites, but that He would fight *where their bodies* (and swords) went! God would defeat their enemies, but He would do it as the Israelites faced the enemy.

The Israelite army marched around Jericho for seven days in silence. They were undoubtedly beseeching God at that time for victory on the seventh day. At the appointed moment, they gave a shout, and the walls of the city fell down. But they still had to go in and *physically possess* the land before victory was complete.

Can you imagine the walls falling, and the jubilant army jumping up and down, saying, "Great job, God! We can see everything now! Okay, God, go get 'em! Finish the battle! Kill 'em, God! Strike them with a lightning bolt! Open the earth and swallow them! Defeat the enemy, God! We beseech You, O, Lord . . ."

As ridiculous as it sounds, that is exactly what many Christians are saying today. They are concerned about abortion and the future of America, and they are praying, but that's all. They are praying, but not acting, and little happens. The abortion mills stay open. The abortionists go on killing.

I am not downplaying the importance of prayer. We *must* beseech God for His help and blessing, for without His intervention we cannot win. He is the "master of breakthrough," who can break through the walls of the enemy. But after we pray and the "spiritual walls" come down, we must do what the Israelites did—occupy enemy territory.

God brought victory when a portion of the Israelites went in and faced the enemy, on the enemy's turf. If we would see God bring victory against abortion, a portion of the church must bodily confront the abortionists head-on.

Gaining Political Clout

The pro-life movement lacks political clout. Most politicians do not take us seriously. Why? Because our actions betray our words. Christians and non-Christians alike who are adamantly against abortion refer to abortion as murder, *but we do not act like it's murder.* Our cries of "murder!" go unheard because our actions are so far removed from our rhetoric.

If a child you love was about to have his arms and legs ripped off, and you could intervene to save him, what would you do? Would you write your Congressman saying, "My little friend is about to be killed, and I ask you to introduce legislation as soon as possible that would prevent such atrocities"?

No! You would do whatever you could to physically intervene and save the life of that child! That is the *appropriate response* to murder.

Well, children we love *are* having their arms and legs torn off, but our response has been grossly inadequate. I am not undermining the validity of writing our Congressmen. I'm saying that many in our ranks must prove to Congress that we believe abortion is murder by *acting* like it's murder. Then laws to stop this holocaust could be passed.

Up until now, the pro-life movement has been like the boy who cried, "Wolf!" We lack credibility. Politicians know how someone *should* respond to murder.

When government officials see people peacefully blockading abortion mills, they begin to take them seriously. When a politician sees good, decent citizens risking arrest and prosecution, he knows they mean business. The strength of their convictions forces him to consider the reasons for their actions and the merits of their arguments.

Creating Social Tension

Even a brief overview of American history will prove that political change usually results from social tension. The birth of America, the end of slavery, women's voting rights, the labor movement, the repeal of the Eighteenth Amendment (which outlawed alcohol), the civil rights movement, the anti-Vietnam War movement, the sexual revolution, the homosexual rights movement, and the feminist movement all testify to one truth: *Whether for good or bad, political change comes after a group of Americans bring enough tension in the nation and pressure on the politicians that the laws are changed.*

Somebody put it this way: Politicians see the light after they feel the heat!

The most famous act of "civil disobedience" in American history was the drafting and signing of the Declaration of Independence. That celebrated day and document were clearly illegal, calling for treason against the British crown.

The "social tension" created on July 4, 1776, and more importantly, the war that followed, resulted in the establishment of possibly the greatest nation ever on earth, except for ancient Israel. No doubt the loyalists, some of them Christians, refused to side with the founding fathers on the grounds that it was a rebellion. I'm glad the revolutionaries won!

Susan B. Anthony and the Suffragette Movement, which secured the right for women to vote, was a street level activist movement. When Susan B. Anthony went to voting booths *demanding* the right to vote, she was arrested and sent to jail. But her actions forced social tension and a national debate on the issue of women's voting rights.

The women won. But had Susan B. Anthony not been overt in her demands, had she not created social and political tension, had she only written letters to her Congressmen, women *still* might not have the right to vote.

The Civil Rights Movement

The best recent example of changing the course of the nation was the black civil rights movement in the late fifties and early sixties, particularly under the leadership of Dr. Martin Luther King, Jr.

By enlisting the black church leadership, and then mobilizing thousands of churchgoers, the civil rights leaders were able to direct people in actions that produced social tension, then political change.

If blacks were forbidden to eat at a given lunch counter, they were trained to sit peacefully at the counter until arrested. If they were forbidden to exercise their First Amendment right to free speech and peaceful assembly, they gathered anyway. If they were told to ride in the back of the bus, they rode in the front. If they were not allowed to register to vote, they went to the registrar and demanded to be registered.

Wherever the boil of segregation existed, they would insert the lance of confrontation, so all the world could see the sickening truth.

Winning with Nonviolence

While some radical groups were inciting violence in the mid to late sixties, the main leadership of the civil rights movement believed in *nonviolence* of word, deed, and heart. Who can forget the sight of water cannons and dogs being turned on defenseless people, including children?

Remember the brutal beatings the Alabama State Police gave the marchers who dared cross the Edmund Pettus Bridge going out of Selma? Those trained in the nonviolent ethic remained true to their vision despite opposition and retaliation.

The peaceful, nonviolent, non-retaliatory *suffering* of the black civil rights activists, many of them Christians, helped win the hearts of millions, and was the catalyst to the Civil Rights Act of 1964, and the Voting Rights Act of 1965. Blacks, willing to suffer and risk arrest in order to stand for what was right, created a tension in the nation that forced politicians to take action.

While the injustice blacks faced was intolerable, can segregation be as bad as murder? Isn't this slaughter of the innocent a far darker evil than segregation ever could be? Isn't the decapitation of millions of defenseless children more barbaric than the sufferings blacks endured?

Why haven't we confronted this bloodshed with a fraction of the sacrifice that blacks made? Because we are afraid, selfish, and blind to the vested interest we have in ending this holocaust.

Pushing the Right Button

The ultimate legal victory for the children will be an amendment to the Constitution, outlawing abortion. Overturning *Roe vs. Wade* would be a step in the right direction, but that would only restore individual states' rights regarding abortion laws. Liberal states like New York, California, and others would become havens where the killing would continue.

We need a paramount Human Life Amendment to bring about a national change. That means we must have a political victory. Pro-lifers have been seeking political victory without success for many years. We have obviously been pushing the wrong buttons.

The winning button—the soft underbelly of the government—has not been pushed. Our founding fathers recognized that soft underbelly when they said the government derives ''its just powers from the consent of the governed.'' When large numbers no longer consent, the government loses its power to govern.

What politicians fear most is social unrest and upheaval. When unrest occurs in small numbers, it can be put down by force. But when unrest and upheaval begin to incorporate hundreds and thousands of people, government officials pay attention. Ultimately, they *desire* to give in to the demands of the disgruntled, so that tranquility can be restored to the realm and they can get on with the business of governing a sleeping nation.

Victory over abortion is possible. All we need is for a remnant of the church to repent and rise up and say, ''No more dead children! We are not going to let you kill innocent babies anymore!'' With the prayers and blessing of others in the church, in harmony with the other avenues of pro-life action discussed, we would see the tide begin to turn.

Victory in Numbers

When I wrote most of this book, I was in jail in Binghamton, New York. Why? Because we did rescue missions in very small numbers and I was the only one with multiple arrests and convictions. Hence, I sat in jail for a few days.

But the entire Binghamton jail system, which can hold about two hundred people, is almost full now. Over 20,000 professing evangelicals and probably three times as many Catholics live in the Binghamton area. Only two abortion mills mar our community. That's 80,000 Roman Catholics and evangelicals against two death camps.

If three percent of that group, just 2400 people, agreed to do multiple sit-ins at the local death camp, what do you think would happen? Probably nothing would happen to us, and we would likely keep the abortion mills from doing their bloody work. Children and mothers would be rescued, and virtually no one would go to jail. We would totally *clog the system*.

The police, the district attorney, the courts, and the jails are not prepared or designed to deal with such huge numbers. And that uprising would only consist of *three percent* of the religious community.

The Only Way to Win

Now imagine people blocking abortion clinics all across the country. Imagine politicians reading in the *New York Times* and *Washington Post* that scores, hundreds, or even thousands of decent, tax-paying citizens in New York City, Washington D.C., St. Louis, Chicago, Philadelphia, and *your town* were demanding an end to the killing.

Envision pastors and priests in jail together for a few days. Imagine the evening news finally beginning to reveal the true horror of abortion because our sacrificial actions *demand* a fair hearing. Think what stirring speeches would be made on the House and Senate floor by politicians who used to be pro-abortion, but who have seen the light—after they felt the heat!

Imagine the political bandwagon forming to amend the Constitution and restore peace, tranquility, and unity to the country. Hear the President eulogizing those courageous Americans who have been willing to risk personal liberty for the justice due their fellow human beings. And see, once and for all, the end of this legalized bloodshed by means of a Constitutional amendment.

I confess, it will take the hand of God for this to happen, but His hand has moved before when others stood in the gap, and attempted what seemed impossible. Why couldn't it happen now? The war *can* be won, and this is what it will take.

Rescue missions are *not* simply *one* part of this battle. The truth is *victory cannot be had without them.*

Without rescues, children continue to die, and mothers continue to be maimed. Without rescues, our obedience to God is incomplete, and His full blessing will continue to be absent. Without them, the political machine will continue to ignore us. Without rescues, our rhetoric is shallow and meaningless. Without righteous, peaceful uprising that demands an end to the killing, America is racing toward divine judgment.

Who will stand in the gap? Who will rise up? Who will the courageous "three percent" be? In a conventional war, the government can draft conscripts to fight. No draft exists in the church. Each one must pray and count the cost himself.

Who Me? Go to Jail?

Will you consider being one on the front line? If enough of us rise up together, the risk is minimal. Even if our numbers are small in the beginning, first and second time offenders are generally treated with leniency. In virtually all cities where large rescues have occurred, even rescuers with multiple arrests spent no time in jail.

Besides, jail is not that bad. They feed you, wash your clothes, and it is a tremendous opportunity to preach the gospel. (You always wanted a jail ministry, right?)

Jail time galvanizes others to be more courageous. The apostle Paul wrote,

> Now I want you to know, brethren, that my circumstances [jail] have turned out for the greater progress of the gospel, so that my imprisonment

> in the cause of Christ has become well known throughout the whole praetorian guard and to everyone else, and that most of the brethren, trusting in the Lord because of my imprisonment, have *far more courage* to speak the word of God without fear—Philippians 1:12-14, italics added.

Going to jail gives fresh vision and courage to others to join you. When I first went to jail to serve a ten-day sentence, eight Christians on the outside were so encouraged, they organized and did a rescue mission. It was exciting. Since Operation Rescue began, thousands of people have participated in rescue missions and hundreds of children have been saved from slaughter.

During and after the 1988 Democratic Convention in Atlanta, several hundred brave men and women decided to confront the enemy on his own territory. They chose to identify with the nameless children being murdered by calling themselves "Baby John Doe" and "Baby Jane Doe." Because they refused to give their own names, the Atlanta rescuers were not released but kept in jail. (See Appendix II for a summary of the events in Atlanta.)

The personal sacrifice of time, money, and energy made by these courageous warriors on the front lines of this war has not gone unnoticed. The hundreds incarcerated in Atlanta have given fresh zeal and vision to the pro-life movement in a way nothing else could. As more people are arrested and willingly spend time in jail, the vision spreads, courage swells, and hope rises in our hearts.

Prime Candidates

God is calling many of you to the front lines of the battle to save children and mothers. And no one person or group is more qualified than another. People from all walks of life have participated in rescues and been arrested—housewives, nurses, pastors, computer programmers, grandparents, college students. All you need is a heart for God, a burden for the children, and a willingness to sacrifice.

Are you a pastor? You have the greatest responsibility for ending this holocaust. Your flock will follow your *example,* not your words.

If you have been inactive in pro-life work, then no doubt your congregation has been basically inactive. If you just preach against abortion, results will be minimal. But if you begin to teach and preach on activism, and then fight for the children and mothers, your sheep will also rise up with courage and follow your example. If you participate in rescue missions, some of your people will undoubtedly follow your lead.

Are you in the ministry full time? If you are, and you have job security, perhaps you could afford to spend a few weeks in jail! As we saw, the apostle Paul's imprisonment inspired others to greater courage in the cause of Christ. (See Philippians 1:12-14.) I can testify my jail time has inspired others to greater depths of sacrifice.

Are you single? If so, you are a prime candidate to be a front-line foot soldier. Your family and financial responsibilities are usually far smaller than those of us who are married and have children. You should seriously consider giving one or two years of your life to this battle. You could spend a few weeks in jail with very few if any repercussions.

As long as you keep your charges to violations or misdemeanors, your career plans will probably not be jeopardized. In fact violations (which are lower than misdemeanors) do not involve fingerprinting or a criminal record. In the past, other social movements with mass arrests indicate that these types of arrests have no effect on a person's career.

But don't take this kind of commitment lightly. There is a price to be paid. Making the decision to be arrested and/or jailed must be weighed carefully beforehand. Each of us must count the cost individually and decide what we're going to do for the children.

We must all take a long hard look at the crisis before us and consider what our part in ending it should be. If many volunteer for the front lines, we can win. If only a few heed the call, we will surely lose the pro-life battle and the lives of millions more children—and the future of our country.

13
Preparing for Action

Lyn Cryderman

Words of Advice
And Encouragement

13
Preparing for Action
Words of Advice and Encouragement

God's love and His shed blood make all people valuable. Whether born, unborn, handicapped, elderly, sinner, or saint, all are made in the image of God. Only the Bible gives us this proper view of man.

Our generation, however, has been thoroughly indoctrinated in humanist thinking. This godless philosophy makes man a mere animal—the chance arrangement of molecules in an evolutionary process.

Under humanism, life is cheap: man has no God-given value and therefore is expendable. Humanism causes people to treat other humans with brutality and contempt—"the survival of the fittest" attitude.

In the pamphlet, *Children... Things We Throw Away?*, Melody Green quotes a doctor who had been doing abortions for twenty years:

> "The first time I felt like a murderer, but I did it again and again . . . Sure, I got hard. Sure, the money was important. And oh, it was an easy thing, once I had taken this step—to see these women as animals and these babies as just tissue."

The church has been poisoned by this mentality. Human life has been greatly devalued in the minds of Christians. The absence of Christians at abortion mills testifies to this.

Franky Schaeffer has said that any community that has an abortion mill standing unchallenged by Christians should have a sign placed over the door reading, "This abortion mill owned and operated with the blessing of the Christian community." Hard words, but true. Unchallenged aborturaries are a disgrace to the Christian community.

Why Rescue Missions?

Prayer is critical in this fight, but prayer without action has resulted in twenty-five million dead children to date. We must put feet to our prayers. God commands, not suggests, that His people *actively defend* the helpless. Sympathy without action is meaningless—only direct action will save lives.

Our actions speak louder than our words. In fact, our actions often betray our words. If we say "abortion is murder!", we must *act* like it is murder by being present at abortion mills and trying to rescue unborn babies from death.

The presence of Christians at abortion mills is demanded because that is where the killing takes place. The command, "Rescue those being led away to death; hold back those staggering toward slaughter" (Proverbs 24:11, NIV) can only be fulfilled by our physical presence at the place of slaughter.

If enough people are involved, no one goes to jail! And if a wave of large rescue missions sweeps the country, politicians will see that we mean business, and the wheels will be set in motion to reverse this holocaust! I *know* it can happen if we are only willing to sacrifice.

We intend to win this war. Child killing *can* be made illegal again. We must fight with that end in mind, knowing that God is fighting with us. As we stir the body of Christ to repentance and action, the gates of hell will not prevail against us.

What's Holding You Back?

God has called us to take a public stand against abortion. We are not only standing for the children and mothers but as witnesses of God's righteous laws. We testify to a rebellious generation that they will give an account to God for their actions on the day of judgment. We stand as witnesses before the hosts of hell that God still has a people who uphold His law and stand against wickedness.

Taking a public stand at an abortion mill is crucial to confronting and exposing the abortion holocaust. Most of the real reasons people don't want to participate in a rescue have nothing to do with Scripture. Are these some of the excuses holding you back?

1. *"I've never done it before."* Most people have never publicly demonstrated or been involved in a sit-in, and we all tend to shy away from new ventures.

2. *"What will people think of me?"* Publicly participating in a rescue can be a real pride-killer for those who would rather preserve their image than look foolish for Jesus' and for the children's sake.

3. *"I don't want to upset anybody."* Many Christians try to avoid the discomfort of confrontation at all costs. They want to be so "loving" that they never make any waves, never point out sin, and never make anyone uncomfortable by standing for what is right.

4. *"I'm afraid of the consequences."* There are risks involved in participating in a rescue. You will probably be arrested by the police, taken to a precinct for processing, and placed in a holding cell. You may have to appear in court and be fined or spend a few days in jail. But look at the rewards, "Blessed are those who have been persecuted for the sake of righteousness, for theirs is the kingdom of heaven" (Matthew 5:10).

You Can Make a Difference

When you and others take a public stand against abortion by blocking the doors of an abortion mill, many positive things happen as a result.

1. *You buy time for the children scheduled to be killed that day.* By sitting in front of an abortuary door, you prevent the personnel from entering and the clients from keeping their appointments. This forces the "clinic" to open late and cuts down on the number of murders they can complete that day. Or it may close down for the *entire day.*

2. *You can save a life!* A pregnant woman coming to the clinic for a pregnancy test or an abortion that day may see the crowd, change her mind, and choose life for her baby.

3. *You give sidewalk counselors the time and opportunity to counsel pregnant women.* Because they are unable to enter the abortuary for their appointment, these women are approached by sidewalk counselors who suggest they consider an alternative to abortion.

4. *You remind local people that children are being killed in their community.* A large rescue shows that there are many people who hate the injustice of murdering innocent children and who will take personal risks to stop the killing.

5. *You help make a rescue a media event.* This helps create social tension and public awareness of the pro-life movement. In addition, a young woman considering abortion may see the coverage on TV or in the newspaper and choose life for her unborn child.

6. *Your presence will bring conviction on others.* Some people who pass by will see the rescue and ask themselves why they aren't taking a stand for the children. This may cause them to join you at this time or on another rescue.

7. *Men, angels, and demons see that God still has people who will stand against wickedness.* You can rest assured that all of heaven—and hell—are watching.

8. *You can witness for the Lord.* Interested people—before, during, and after the rescue—will ask why you are willing to risk arrest for this cause. This is a perfect opportunity to share your faith in Jesus Christ and the reason for your obedience to God's commands.

9. *You make others aware of the horrors of abortion.* Your presence at an abortion mill gives sidewalk counselors opportunities to hand out literature to pregnant women and passersby, helping to re-educate them. Many people are still unaware of what really happens in an abortion.

10. *Some results are not obvious.* You may never know (until eternity) about the lives that are changed and the children who are saved as a result of your selfless participation in a rescue mission.

The Secret to Victory

The Lord Jesus Christ is the foundation and life source of Operation Rescue. We know that without Him we can do nothing. A personal relationship with Jesus Christ is essential to victory—both personally and corporately.

If you want to win in this battle, make communion with Christ your first priority. As you reach Him in prayer, He will endow you with power. As you fellowship with Him in the secret place, you will bear His authority in the public place. Without this intimacy, you and I will be lifeless and powerless to deal with the crisis at hand.

Communion with Christ should be a way of life. A half hour or hour with God in the morning is critical, but it must not stop there. Consistently abide in Him, and allow Him to abide in you. We need an attitude of total dependency—"praying without ceasing."

> Pray in the Spirit on all occasions with all kinds of prayers and requests. With this in mind, be alert and always keep on praying for all the saints—Ephesians 6:18, NIV.

Battling the Enemy

Any front-line soldier in this battle against abortion must be spiritually prepared. Besides human adversaries, we have spiritual forces working against us.

> For our struggle is not against flesh and blood, but against the rulers, against the authorities, against the powers of this dark world and against the spiritual forces of evil in the heavenly realms— Ephesians 6:12, NIV.

Our battle is not only against the unscrupulous doctors, the greedy clinic owners, the misguided feminists, or the biased media. We are fighting the unseen forces of ignorance and apathy along with the spiritual forces of murder and child sacrifice.

Satan receives the bodies of these innocent children as blood sacrifices offered to him in worship. (See Psalm 106:37.) But he has cleverly hidden his bloodthirty lust behind a deception so powerful and so organized that an entire nation has believed it.

Satan will not give up this stronghold without a fight to the very end. Anyone who enters this conflict must be prepared for the spiritual battle of his or her life.

Are you a praying person? If not, stop! Don't even start in this ministry because, once you begin, you will be sorely tried by the enemy. The devil will seek to bring havoc into your life, so don't be surprised when it happens—expect it. Anger, depression, domestic conflict, persecution—the attack may come in any number of ways. But it will come.

If you pray, you need not fear. God will take you through all of Satan's schemes, and having done all, you will stand. If you don't pray, you won't be able to withstand the attack. You'll become discouraged and will suddenly be "led in another direction." Avoid this by much praying.

Standing Your Ground

If we pray, we will succeed. If we don't pray, we will fail. How will we fail? *We will give up.*

Lay your hand to the plow with a commitment to go forward until we win or die trying. Perseverance means to pursue an undertaking in spite of opposition, negative influences, and disappointment. Realize that at times you will feel like quitting or think that your efforts are all but useless.

The early Christians who were sent to the lions were victorious because they kept the faith. We, too, are victorious when we stand unyieldingly in the face of adversity for these little children and their mothers. We are victorious if we stand faithfully, whether we accomplish much or little.

Do not put any hope or trust in your own strength or resources for they are futile in this spiritual battle.

> Give us aid against the enemy, for the help of man is worthless. With God we will gain the victory, and he will trample down our enemies—Psalm 108:12,13, NIV.

We will have to go to battle, but we will go in God's strength. If we put our faith in Him and not in ourselves, He will bring the victory.

How to Pray

The truths in this book are like a garden hose—dry and of no benefit until used to transport life-giving water. As you pray, the living water of God's Spirit will give life and power to these truths. The flow of God's Spirit will rise and fall in relation to *your prayer life,* thus determining your effectiveness and the blessings these truths will have on people.

Scripture exhorts us to "seek the Lord and His strength;

seek His face continually'' (Psalms 105:4). Seek Him for His wisdom, His guidance, His provision, His power, and, most of all, His presence. As we do, His purposes will unfold and come to pass before our eyes, abundantly above all that we can ask or even think.

If you are faithful in prayer, God will raise you up as a standard bearer of His righteousness, and you will take ground for the kingdom of God. Remember, God is more interested in halting this atrocity than you are. Avail yourself of His power and blessing by constantly seeking His face.

1. Pray for the women in your city contemplating having an abortion. Ask the Lord to send people across their path who can bring them to the truth. Ask the Holy Spirit to convict the hearts of these young women and cause them to choose life for their child.

2. Pray that the Holy Spirit will convict the hearts of the doctors and nurses and owners of the abortion clinics. Seek God for the salvation of medical personnel that will result in a mass exodus of staff from the abortuaries of America.

3. Pray against the spirit of murder that has permeated our land through the legalization of abortion.

4. Pray against the forces of deception that perpetrate lies through the liberal media, Planned Parenthood, the National Organization for Women, etc.

5. Pray for a national outcry against the horrors of abortion that will result in a constitutional amendment.

6. Pray for God to touch the hearts of Christian that they will act according to God's Word and do their part to end this slaughter.

7. Pray for a spirit of repentance to sweep over God's people. Ask the Lord to send prophets to call the body of Christ to repent of our apathy and disobedience during this holocaust.

Turning the Heart of the Nation

God's law can never be made null and void by men. *Never!* Christians must rise up and obey God's command to rescue the children regardless of men's edicts that prohibit us and protect the killers. As we count the cost and obey God, He will honor our obedience by turning the heart of this nation back to the children.

I truly believe we can win this battle, but first a mighty repentance must sweep through the church. We must repent of an apathy so vile that it has allowed millions and millions of children to be slaughtered right under our noses—while we didn't even lift a finger to try and stop it.

We must repent of a selfishness so deep, that like the Levite and the priest, we have passed by on our way to truly "spiritual activities" while children died in the ditch of abortion mills. This grievous sin must be repented of.

As we repent of selfishness and take up our cross, we will become warriors that will not be defeated. The angels of heaven will fight with us, and the gates of hell will not prevail against us. Children and mothers will be saved. Abortion will be made illegal again! The heart of this nation will again turn toward righteousness and compassion.

In whatever you do, your attitude must be one of brokenness and humility. We cannot self-righteously condemn the abortionist and the politician without first realizing that we *all* share in the guilt. In fact, our guilt is greater than most because we have more truth than most. As Christians, *we*, not the police or the politicians, are the salt of the earth.

We must not portray a bitter or haughty heart, but a contrite one. Then we can call people to repentance *with* us, not call *them* to repentance while we watch in glee. If our spirit is loving and not hateful, repentant and not arrogant, forgiving and not condemning, we will win the sympathy in our nation for the cause of the children.

Good Soldiers

As part of our preparation for action, each of us must look into our hearts and lives and ask ourselves, "What kind of soldier am I?"

What are some of the characteristics of a warrior that we must have in order to be victorious?

1. Warriors are prepared to sacrifice. They are willing to give up what is rightfully theirs in a time of peace in order to gain the victory in a time of war.
2. Warriors sacrifice for fellow soldiers.
3. Warriors have self-discipline.
4. Warriors take orders and carry them out to the end.
5. Warriors should be noble and trustworthy.
6. Warriors expect the enemy to malign them, ridicule them, fight against them, and lie about them.
7. Warriors know that if they don't defeat the enemy, the enemy will defeat them. There is no stalemate, no neutral ground.
8. Warriors don't run from conflict; they run to it.
9. Warriors fight to win!
10. Warriors are prepared to die.

Are you a good soldier (warrior) of the Lord Jesus Christ?

The apostle Paul wrote:

> Suffer [endure] hardship with me, as a good soldier of Christ Jesus. No soldier in active service entangles himself in the affairs of everyday life, so that he may please the one who enlisted him as a soldier—2 Timothy 2:3,4.

In order to endure hardship and be a good warrior in this fight, you must do one thing—*die to yourself.* Only then will you be able to persevere. Only then will you be willing to make the depth of sacrifice that is necessary to fight for the children.

We must repent of our unwillingness to endure hardship and our desire to flee when tough times come. Then God can mold us into warriors who persevere in this battle.

H. W. Beecher said: "Victories that are easy are cheap. Those only are worth having which come as the result of hard fighting."

Live For Jesus

Why are we trying to win the war against abortion? To make points with God? To gain the praise of our fellow Christians? To show what kind of stuff we are made of? If we are, then we are fighting for the wrong reasons.

Our first and foremost motivation must be to obey God and to save the precious children He created.

The apostle Paul wrote: "For to me, to live is Christ" (Philippians 1:21). This theme occurs throughout the writings of this great apostle. His life, his affections, his thoughts, his goals, his desires were all bound up and found in the person of the Lord Jesus Christ.

While Paul knew he had to reach people with the gospel, the people were not his life—Jesus was. With Jesus as his Lord, Paul did certain things for people, but those he served were not the center of his life.

There is *no life,* no life-giving power, in the abortion battle. If you make abortion your life focus, you will die as surely as a man who fights in a war without taking time to eat and drink.

We cannot warn against this snare enough. Your heart must be filled with a love for Jesus more than a hatred for child killing. Your mind must focus on thoughts of Christ not constantly dwell on the injustice that is happening to children.

As soldiers, we must obey our Commander's orders in this principle. He is first. He is our all. He is the captivator of our hearts. Otherwise we will become mean, hateful, bitter, and finally of little or no effect in this battle. We will burn out.

Guard Your Heart

The apostle Paul made great sacrifices because of his love for Jesus. He worked with an eye toward the day when he would stand and give an account to the King of Kings. Likewise, we will make great sacrifices for children, but ultimately it must be for the love of Christ.

If we put the work first in our hearts instead of Christ, it becomes idolatry. God will not tolerate idolatry even when the idol is ministry. He is a jealous God; hence you must constantly guard your heart and keep it focused on Christ. He is the lover and keeper of our souls.

With Christ as our source and strength, we will be empowered to do His work. We will enjoy His presence and the joy and peace He brings. We will have the will to persevere when everything around us appears to be crumbling. We will have an anointing to combat the forces of hell. When bad press comes (and be prepared, it will come), it won't devastate us for we are not living for the praise of men. We are living for the day when God commends us for our works.

With an Eye Toward Eternity

Let us, therefore, proceed in this work. Let us look to Jesus, seek His face, obey His commands, and not balk because of the cost it brings to us personally. Let us be good soldiers. Jesus laid down His life for us; we must be willing to lay down our lives for Him.

I leave you in the hands of the God of all grace who is able to keep you from falling and to use you for His purposes, above all that you ask or think. Stand for God's righteous precepts. Reach out to the mothers in this hour of crisis. Speak up for the innocent children who can't speak up for themselves, and intervene to save their lives.

Persevere in this work with an eye toward eternity. For if your work survives the fire of God, you will receive a reward.

> For no one can lay any foundation other than the one already laid, which is Jesus Christ. If any man builds on this foundation using gold, silver, costly stones, wood, hay, or straw, his work will be shown for what it is, because the Day will bring it to light. It will be revealed with fire, and the fire will test the quality of each man's work. If what he has built survives, he will receive his reward—1 Corinthians 3:11-14, NIV.

Live in truth and obey the light that you have, so that on that awesome day, when the hidden things and the motives of men's hearts are laid bare, you will hear Him say, "Well done, thou good and faithful servant." Nothing else will matter.

Bless those who seek You, Lord Jesus. Amen.

Appendixes

I

What You Can Expect

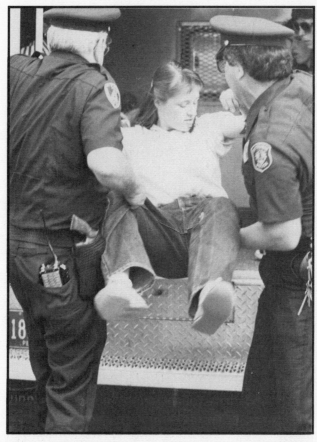

Jeanne Robinson

Participating in a
Rescue Mission

I

What You Can Expect

Participating in a Rescue Mission

Now that you have the biblical motivation for rescuing children, God may be speaking to you about organizing or participating in a rescue.

If you are a pastor or pro-life leader in your area, Operation Rescue can provide step by step guidelines for organizing a local rescue. See the *Information* section of this book for the materials you will need.

If you are a lay person who feels called to the front lines, then you probably have many questions. Like: How do I become involved? How much will it cost in time, energy, sacrifice, and money? How do I prepare for a rescue mission?

These questions are difficult to answer because each community is different and each rescue has its own unique set of circumstances. For information about participating in a rescue in your area, call your local pro-life organization to find out if and when they are planning a rescue. If there is no local pro-life group organizing rescues, you may want to take the initiative and plan one. Make sure, however, that you have the blessing of your pastor (unless you are a pastor!).

If you want to be involved in one of our large national rescues, contact the Operation Rescue office. (See *Information* for address and phone number.)

Participating in a rescue mission usually involves four steps:

1. The rally
2. The rescue
3. The arrest
4. Court proceedings

The Rally

As plans for a rescue mission in your city or community begin to crystalize, pastors and other pro-life leaders will announce the date and time for the rally. This rally is usually held several days or the evening before the rescue. The rally is very important because you will be informed of the specifics of the rescue: the site, the time, what to wear, what to bring or not bring, how to respond to police and the media, transportation to and from the site, and many other details.

Speakers. The rally sets the tone for the rescue and helps prepare your heart with an attitude of humility and repentance. A local pastor or pro-life leader will challenge and encourage rescuers and potential rescuers with a message from God's Word.

Those who have participated in past rescues will also address the crowd, explaining their personal and often gradual involvement in the war against child killing. You will discover that they are ordinary people, much like yourself. Not long ago they may have been struggling with the same apathy or frustration that you may detect in yourself. But they believed God and moved beyond themselves to actually do something about the atrocity of abortion. You can, too.

"We've been involved in pro-life work for years," said one middle-aged couple who addressed a recent rally in Pittsburgh. "During that time we've witnessed over ten thousand women pass our picket lines, refuse to be dissuaded by pro-life literature, and enter abortion clinics to have their children killed. Over ten thousand!

"Just picketing was not the answer. Sure, a few here and there turned away, but thousands met an untimely death at the hands of the abortionists. But when we had a rescue and sealed off the entrance to the death chamber, many mothers ultimately chose life for their children."

Prayer. The rally is also a place where evangelical pastors, charismatics, and Catholic brothers and sisters can unite in prayer against the strongholds of Satan in that particular locality. Praying against the powers of immorality, murder, greed, deception, and convenience that grip your city is an important part of the rally. Specific petition should also be made for the women who are contemplating abortion, for their families and boyfriends, for the abortionists, for the sidewalk counselors, for the media, and for the police.

Training. Rescue training is also an important part of the rally. You may be asked to *role play* situations that you will encounter at the rescue site. Potential rescuers will be asked to blockade the door to an imaginary abortuary. What happens if a pregnant woman decides to push her way through the rescuers to get to the door? What do you say if a media representative approaches you with a question or antagonizes you for remaining silent? You may even practice how to go limp as part of your preparation for being carried away by police officers the next day.

Because every situation is different, tactics may change from one rescue to the next. The best way for you to be prepared is to pay close attention to the information and instructions presented by the leaders and crowd marshalls at the rally.

Registration. Before you leave the rally, you will be asked to register for the actual rescue if you have not already done so. The pro-life leadership in your city will want the participants on a mailing list to keep you updated and informed of any court proceedings or future rescues.

You will also be asked to carefully read and sign the following pledge (or one similar to it):

Pledge for On-Site Participation

I understand the critical importance of Operation Rescue being unified, peaceful, and free of any actions or words that would appear violent or hateful to those watching the event on TV or reading about it in the newspaper.

I realize that some pro-abortion elements of the media desire to discredit Rescues *(and then the whole pro-life movement)* and focus on a side issue, in order to avoid the central issue at hand—murdered children.

Hence, I understand that for the *children's sake,* each Rescue must be orderly and above reproach.

Therefore...

I will cooperate with the spirit and goals of Operation Rescue, as explained by the leadership.

I commit to be peaceful and nonviolent in both word and deed.

Should I be arrested, I will not struggle with police in any way (whether deed or tongue), but remain polite and passively limp, remembering that mercy triumphs over judgment.

I will follow the instructions of the Operation Rescue crowd control marshals.

I understand that certain individuals will be appointed to speak to the media, the police, and the women seeking abortion. I will not take it upon myself to yell out to anyone, but will continue singing and praying with the main group, as directed.

I sign this pledge, having seriously considered what I do, and with the determination and will to persevere by the grace of God.

Signature_____   Date_____

Last-Minute Preparations

As the day of the rescue approaches, it's only natural to have some questions about how to prepare. Although every rescue is different and involves specific instructions, here are some practical guidelines that apply to most rescues.

What should my attitude be? It is most important that you come in a spirit of humility and unity, demonstrating a "we" mentality and not a "me" mentality. Remember, one purpose for coming together is to repent for our inactivity on behalf of the unborn. If you're there to get a kick out of getting arrested, your motivation is seriously wrong. Our only reason for doing a rescue is to save children in obedience to God's Word.

What should I wear? Operation Rescue is a grassroots movement of respectable, upright, moral citizens, and we should dress like it. When bystanders, police, newspaper reporters, cameramen, and anchorpersons arrive on the scene, we want them to perceive us as "middle America," not some lunatic fringe demonstrating for our own rights.

Weather permitting, jeans or comfortable slacks and a nice shirt are ideal. Wear an old pair of tennis shoes since they're likely to get scuffed up on the sidewalk. You may need a light jacket while sitting in the cool of the morning or in the shadow of city skyscrapers. Avoid wearing T-shirts or hats that display advertising.

Pastors who normally wear clerical collars (or any pastor who feels comfortable wearing one) are encouraged to do so. All other pastors should wear a shirt, tie, and sports jacket with jeans or rugged pants. If the media interviews you, the cameraman will only shoot you from the waist up. Pro-life doctors, nurses, and other health professionals are encouraged to wear their uniforms.

Don't wear anything that you wouldn't mind getting dragged away in, depending on how the police are equipped to handle the crowds.

What should I bring? Hopefully, you will be blockading the entrance of an abortion clinic for several hours. To make the hard, concrete sidewalk more bearable, you may want to bring a stadium cushion, a towel, some newspapers wrapped in plastic, or some suitable pad to sit on. Gospel tracts or a pocket Bible or New Testament may come in handy since many rescuers have had opportunity to share Christ with interested passersby, arresting officers, and jail guards.

Bring enough money to pay for public transportation to your car or meeting site, especially if the number of rescuers is so great that police need to process you at several precincts spread throughout your city. Ten dollars is usually more than enough money to have on hand. You may want to have sufficient change for phone calls.

What about food and drink? Remember that once you sit down in front of a clinic you may be there for a while. Some rescuers have elected to fast during the day. Or you may want to bring granola bars, trail mix, or some other snack. On especially hot days, small juice "box drinks," apples, grapes, and other fruit can prevent dehydration. Chewing gum will also keep your mouth from drying out.

To prevent your need of restroom facilities, you may want to stop drinking after midnight on the eve of the rescue. Take just a few sips of water in the morning and be sure to use the bathroom before you leave for the rescue site. In the case of a six or eight-hour seige, several people at a time can leave the site to use a nearby restroom.

What should I not bring? Do not bring money for bond or bail. By telling the authorities that *no one* is posting bond or bail, we force them to jail all of us (which would place a crushing burden on the already overcrowded penal system) or to release all of us.

In case of rain, do not bring umbrellas, since they pose a potential risk to your fellow rescuers. Rain ponchos or rain jackets are a much better choice. In a pinch a large plastic trash bag will also keep you dry.

Do not bring picket signs to the rescue. Like umbrellas, they could harm your fellow pro-lifers. The leadership will provide a limited number of signs that will effectively communicate the message of the rescue.

Check with the leadership on whether or not to bring pro-life tracts since they may want only the designated sidewalk counselors to have approved literature.

How do I get to the rescue site? At the rally you will be told where to meet the next day. Rescuers will gather at a rendezvous point that may be a few blocks or a few miles from the abortion mill. At the meeting place, maps will be given to drivers. Media people who have been contacted can follow, but it is not wise to inform them of the actual rescue site. In fact, making a general announcement of the targeted abortuary is discouraged, and divulging specific details should be on a "need to know" basis only.

Once everyone is present at the rendezvous point, leaders will make last minute announcements, pray, and then everyone will move out on foot, or in cars, vans, buses, etc. Rescuers should plan to arrive one-half hour to an hour before the abortuary is scheduled to open.

At the Rescue Site

Upon arriving at the abortuary, rescuers should position themselves around the door (or doors). Once seated, the group will pray, repent, and sing as pastors or other pro-life leaders intermittently address the rescuers and others who have assembled. When clinic employees arrive for work, rescue spokesmen will politely inform them that no babies will be killed as long as the rescuers are there.

If the abortion clinic leases space in a building that also rents to other businesses, the owners may become visibly upset at the prospect of losing a day's business. A designated spokesman should politely and tactfully explain that you are not there to shut down their business, but they must be aware of the risks involved in renting a building that also allows abortionists to continue their bloody practices. In this way you can make other tenants aware of the fact that women are being exploited and innocent babies are being killed on the premises.

It is important to expose the abortion mill's true work— murder. Many "clinics," eager for good public relations, employ more innocuous names like "women's health services" or "women's reproductive services." Pastors and pro-life leaders can educate the bystanders and the assembling crowd about the atrocities of abortion that are being perpetrated behind that nice office front.

When clients arrive. Sidewalk counselors should be positioned on the outside fringe of all the action, alertly looking for women who may be heading toward the abortuary for an appointment. These counselors should not be distracted by the rescue or the arrest of the rescuers.

When it is time for the clinic to open, some women scheduled for abortions will see the crowd assembled and not even approach the rescue site. Sidewalk counselors will have opportunity to share information, alternatives, and literature with these women. It is at this point that many children are rescued from impending death.

This incident is typical of what happens. During one rescue, a sidewalk counselor approached a young woman who had come for her scheduled abortion. When the counselor asked if she was aware of the medical facts concerning the procedure, the woman said no. After reading pro-life literature for ten minutes, she said, "I can't do this. It's terrible!" She made an appointment with the local pro-life crisis pregnancy organization and is getting the help she needs to give life to her child.

Many other women arrive, see the crowd, the TV cameras, and the police, and walk away from the clinic. Some receive pro-life literature from counselors, and many never return to have their children murdered.

Other women, especially those accompanied by boyfriends who are pressuring them, may refuse to be turned aside. If a woman or a couple approaches the abortuary and tries to wade through the sea of rescuers to get to the door, remain peaceful and simply lock arms together. Rescuers should never touch a client, a clinic employee, or an arresting officer.

At one rescue, a couple began stepping on rescuers in an attempt to get to the entrance. One rescuer put up her hand to protect herself from getting stepped on, and the woman trying to enter the clinic filed an assault charge. A few days later when the plaintiff never appeared in court, the judge totally dismissed the charges. During a second rescue in that same city, legal counsel advised rescuers to stand or kneel and lock arms to keep clients from entering the building and to prevent assault charges from being filed.

How to handle the media. At some point the media will be notified of your location and the nature of the protest. The area may soon be swarming with newspaper reporters, photographers, cameramen, and TV anchorpersons. Operation Rescue believes in exercising wisdom before the media and the world, therefore, designated spokespersons should be assigned to talk with media representatives.

Reporters, of course, will approach any participant for a story. At this point, you should follow the instructions given to you by the leadership at the rally. Sometimes rescuers are instructed to refer media people to designated spokespersons, or you may have the liberty to speak within certain guidelines. Obedience to leadership is very important in this area. Some reporters will try to illicit off-the-cuff remarks from participants in an effort to discredit the rescue.

When the police arrive. The police may discover you on their early morning patrol, or they may be notified by abortion clinic personnel. The officers will probably be stunned by the sight of dozens or even hundreds of average citizens who are peacefully assembled and blocking an abortion clinic at such an early hour.

The element of surprise definitely works on behalf of the rescuers. Most police departments, especially ones in smaller communities, have never dealt with the large numbers that participate in a rescue mission. For a time, you can continue to peacefully protest the slaughter of the unborn while police consult their chain of command and work out a strategy.

At some point, the commanding officer on the scene will probably speak with your leaders, notifying them of the consequences involved in blocking the door of the clinic. Or, police may just make a general announcement of warning and then begin arresting. Charges may be creating a fire hazard, blocking an entrance, trespassing, or obstructing pedestrian traffic.

When you're arrested. You may feel somewhat shaken when you see police reinforcements show up with police vans or buses. Yes, you really are going through with this! Remember that courage is not the absence of fear, but a will to do what is right in spite of your fears. Pastors may encourage rescuers to lay hands on one another and pray that God stirs courage in each others' hearts.

Your leaders will have instructed you to go passively limp when the arrests begin—don't resist, but don't assist, either. The longer it takes for police to remove you, the longer the abortion clinic stays closed. Time becomes the key factor in saving lives that were scheduled for certain death that morning. Also, we don't want to assist with our removal from a place where children will be killed.

The commanding officer may give the group a five-minute warning to vacate the premises, after which arrests will begin. Police vans pull up, and the arresting officers begin dragging or carrying rescuers to the vehicles.

In New York, where Operation Rescue leadership had met with the police department prior to the rescue, the law enforcement officials were prepared to carry people on stretchers to awaiting buses. Police cordially asked rescuers to get on stretchers and took them away without incident. This tactic may, in fact, buy *more* time for the children.

Police departments in some cities may not be as well-equipped to handle a mass demonstration. In one city, police grabbed rescuers by one arm and unceremoniously dragged them across the sidewalk, over the curb, and onto the street. A number of male rescuers were manhandled, but most of the women, including expectant mothers and white-haired grandmothers, were carried to the police vehicles.

Remember that police are people with all sorts of personalities. Whether you encounter officers who are arrogant or amiable, respect their position regardless of their personality. When they left home this morning, they probably didn't expect to be hoisting bodies onto buses for several hours. Since they'll be working harder today than they have in a long time, make allowance for their annoyance.

Once seated in a police van or bus, maintain an attitude of repentance. Instead of becoming argumentative or antagonistic, remain quiet and prayerful. You will discover that many policemen and policewomen are often pro-life. If so, you might share how Christ changed your life and explain why you are rescuing children. You may find that God has been sending other laborers across their paths to sow precious seed that you can now water.

At the Jail

At the precinct, the police may or may not separate the men from the women and begin processing rescuers. Usually, you'll be arrested on a minor charge, which does not include fingerprinting. Depending on the police department, you may be frisked. If this does happen, women will be frisked by policewomen. If you are charged with a misdemeanor, you will fingerprinted. The charges, however, may be reduced later.

While in jail, continue to maintain an attitude of repentance. You may be relieved now that the arrest is over, but remember why you are there. Check with the other rescuers to make sure everyone is all right. Have a time of joint prayer and singing. Be sensitive to the officers who are busy doing their jobs, and don't barrage them with questions. If God provides an opportunity to share with them, do so graciously.

When one jail matron was processing dozens of women rescuers in a holding area, a few concerned Christians engaged this woman in conversation. Before leaving the holding area, the matron asked for prayer for a physical need in her life. Several women laid hands on her through the bars while the entire group lifted their voices to God in prayer.

It is extremely important that you follow every detail of the instructions given you by the rescue leadership concerning the arrest and release procedures. This is no time to take off like the Lone Ranger. Unity at this point is crucial.

When you're released. After the leadership is assured that everyone is charged with the same offense, you will be asked to sign your citation and you will be released. If police have trumped up charges on just a few rescuers to make examples of them, the entire group acting as a unit can use leverage in stating, "We're all released or no one is released." Not many police departments want the additional burden of having to house and feed dozens, scores, or even hundreds of pro-lifers.

Check with rescue leadership before leaving for your car or meeting site. In most cases, you will be released a short time after your arrest. It may take an hour or a few hours. The inconvenience and time is a small price to pay for saving lives that were scheduled for certain death that day.

You may be given a citation when you are released, or you may be contacted by mail. Whatever the charges, you should always plead *not guilty*. The pro-life leadership in your area will be consulting with lawyers on the appropriate legal steps. You will probably be notified by mail as soon as information is available on court proceedings.

Court Proceedings

You will be notified by the authorities concerning the date you are to appear in court. Don't be intimidated by court proceedings. Remember that child killing and the conscience of the community are on trial and *not you*.

It is important that everyone who is charged follow the instructions of the rescue leadership. If you all respond to the charges in the same way, you show a unified front that creates strength in many ways.

If found guilty, you will probably be fined. We recommend not paying it, as a matter of principle. By refusing to pay the fine, you force the judge to deal with these children as people and not simply as an issue. You are preventing murder, but he is fining you for trespassing or some other charge. If you refuse to pay the fine, the judge cannot ignore the fact that the lives of "little" people are involved.

If all of you are fined and refuse to pay, you should ask for a time when you can all turn yourselves in as a group. Go together to the judge and explain that you still cannot in good conscience pay the fine. Then let him do with you as he wills. You may have to spend a few days in jail for doing so, but it is time well spent. You will never be the same.

My pastor participated in a rescue, was tried, found guilty, and fined. He refused to pay the fine. The judge was quite perplexed and very uncomfortable about sentencing Pastor Little to ten days in jail. (He served six with time off for good behavior.) Soon after handing down this sentence, the judge confided to a friend that sentencing good people to jail was more than he could bear. He wrote his letter of resignation and stepped down from the bench.

You never know what effect your stand for righteousness will have on other people. Just be bold, be strong, and take courage, for the Lord is with you—and the outcome is in His hands.

II

A Grassroots Movement

Lyn Cryderman

People With a Purpose

II

A Grassroots Movement

People With a Purpose

The following two accounts appeared in the "May 1988 Pro-Life Newsbrief" published by Project Life of Binghamton, New York. Gary Leber is the managing editor.

Operation Rescue: A Week of Victory!

Over 800 people came from all over the United States and Canada to participate in the largest and most successful series of rescue missions in pro-life history. During the five day period from May 2 through 6, 1988, the Greater New York Metropolitan area and Long Island were the scenes of massive, peaceful direct action as rescuers surrounded abortion mill doors with their bodies, making entrance impossible.

No children died nor were women exploited at any location where a rescue was held. Many mothers ultimately chose life instead of abortion for their children.

On the first day, 503 people, including a Catholic bishop, two monsignors, fifteen priests, four nuns, a Greek Orthodox priest and a deacon, two Jewish rabbis, and over twenty ministers of various evangelical denominations were arrested for saving lives.

The rescue, led by Randall Terry, commenced at 8:00 a.m. as the door was reached and people sat down by the hundreds around the abortuary and began to read prayers and sing hymns and patriotic songs. No violence occurred.

The police began arriving as well as about sixty pro-abortion protesters. "Open the clinic!" they shouted. "Arrest them!" Police then brought in barricades to keep the pro-abortion protesters from intermingling with the rescuers. Their fury increased as they were kept away from the clinic.

The pro-abortionists chanted, "Racist, sexist, anti-gay, born-again bigots, go away!" and "Operation Rescue, that's a lie, you don't care if women die!"

Arrest totals for the four day period amounted to 1647 with over 800 people participating in the rescues.

Sharing In Christ's Suffering

Beth Davey, who participated in the Manhattan rescue, provides a sidewalk view and insight into the feelings a rescuer experiences.

"Arrest them! Arrest them!" The angry chants hurled like weapons from the jeering crowd fell painlessly on the peaceful gathering of hundreds of pro-life supporters. But the vengeance of the crowd suddenly transfixed me to another place, another angry mob 2,000 years ago. "Crucify Him! Crucify Him!"

Never had I understood the Lord's command to "take up your cross and follow Me" as I did that day. As a crowd marshall, I was stationed between the screaming protestors and the sea of people in front of me who sat in prayerful obedience. A wooden barricade and several police officers separated us from the protestors' growing fury. Louder and louder they screamed, the crescendo of their epithets drowning out the leader's voice, but not the songs of the rescuers raised in praise.

I pictured the long and painful journey of Christ as He struggled down a gauntlet of insults and jeers on His way to Calvary. I remembered the piercing crown that adorned His head—a mocking testimony to His "failed" kingdom. Yet the pain did not turn Him aside to compromise. The humiliation did not collapse His resolve to obedience. Jesus knew that victory over sin depended on His total dedication to doing God's will. We are proof of that victory.

On that damp and rainy morning in Manhattan, hate was not returned with hate—victory! Lovers of life felt the power and strength of God—victory! No killing took place—victory! God was glorified and truth upheld—victory!

People with a Purpose

Pastor Keith Tucci of Greater Pittsburgh Word and Worship Fellowship participated in the New York rescues and tells what he saw happening both on and off the street.

The rescuers represented a wide cross-section of Americans. Average people of all ages and from all walks of life showed up on behalf of the unborn. Participants ranged from teenagers to grandparents, indicating that this is a grassroots movement.

During a rescue one day, I said to someone, "If you look across the street at our opponents, that's not middle America over there. But the people in this rescue include yuppies, blue-collar workers, white collar workers, entrepreneurs, welfare people, poor people, rich people, blacks, whites, and Hispanics—people from all walks of life."

The attitude that prevailed among the rescuers was submissive yet military and obligatory. We woke up at five-thirty in the morning, got ready, and followed orders. As the rescuers headed to the rescue site on the subways and buses, we felt a sense of purpose. We were a people of destiny at that moment.

For many of us, that was very important—especially for those who were frustrated with pro-life work. We needed to be able to say, "Today I'm going to save a life, and in the process of saving a life, I'm going to have an opportunity to share Jesus with the lost."

I think more people were saved by accident during Operation Rescue in New York than an evangelistic team of a thousand would have gotten saved on purpose. The gospel was talked about, and it was demonstrated. I don't mean it was demonstrated by sitting down in front of the abortion clinic—it was demonstrated by the way the rescuers cared about people.

Many rescuers didn't just have a zeal over the abortion issue—they had a zeal for God. They loved people. I saw pro-lifers at Operation Rescue reach out to pregnant girls, drug addicts, and the people in the porno districts. They invited street people to come to their hotel rooms to take showers. They bought them lunch and ministered to them.

Then it really hit me. Unborn babies are people. If you care about people, you've got to care about the unborn. If you care about them, then it's natural to care about all the needy of this world.

A spirit of humility, meekness, and cooperation permeated the rescuers and made us all one. I think most people left New York drawn closer to the Lord whether they were evangelicals, pentecostals, denominationals, or Roman Catholics. I don't think anyone felt they were compromising any tenets of their faith to be there. In fact, people were strengthened in the Word of God and in their commitment to Christ. People found greater boldness to share their faith and to stand up for righteousness wherever they went that week. And best of all—Jesus was lifted up.

Over 4000 Arrests

During the one hundred day period between May 1 and early August, 1988, over 4000 arrests resulted from direct action campaigns organized or inspired by Operation Rescue. Not one of these arrests involved verbal or physical violence of any kind on the part of the rescuers.

Rescues took place in cities across the country, including Dobbs Ferry, Buffalo, and Rochester, New York; Pittsburgh, Philadelphia, and Harrisburg, Pennsylvania; Kansas City; Portland, Oregon; Jackson, Mississippi; and Tallahassee, Florida.

The following three news reports appeared in the "June 1988 Pro-Life Newsbrief" published by Operation Rescue.

Operation Rescue—Jackson, Mississippi

On May 14, over 150 pro-lifers gathered to pray, picket, and participate in Mississippi's first rescue mission for the unborn. By 6:45 a.m., over sixty rescuers had blocked all three entrances to the abortuary in order to save babies who were scheduled to die that morning. Shortly after 7:00 a.m., the abortion mill's employees showed up, demanding that they return to their usual picketing area where eighty or more pro-lifers were already manning picket signs or counseling women coming for abortions.

While the rescuers were blocking the entrances, at least half of the abortion-bound mothers were turned away from the death chamber. Police did not return in sufficient numbers to deal with rescuers until 9:15 a.m. When the protestors refused to leave, arrests began.

Among the arrestees was Dr. Beverly McMillan, a former abortionist, whose testimony was seen in the film *Eclipse of Reason*. McMillan was the first ex-abortionist to be arrested for attempting to save babies, and she is the wife of the organizer of the rescue, Roy McMillan.

Also, Detective Joe Daniels, an officer in the Child Protection Division of the Jackson Police Department, after completing his paperwork, which read: "Subject was arrested trespassing at an abortion clinic in an attempt to prevent the massacre of unborn children," typed out his letter of resignation. Daniels explained later that, as pro-lifers prayed for him, he realized he was compromising his Christian beliefs, saying, "I've failed God miserably."

New Yorkers to the Rescue

In the wake of Operation Rescue in New York, the freshly invigorated pro-lifers of the New York City area staged the largest "local" rescue to date.

The Women's Medical Pavilion in Westchester County, located just north of New York City, was barricaded by 174 rescuers on June 11. Jesse Lee, one of the rescue organizers, said preparations worked "with surgical precision." The rescuers occupied the doorway from 7:15 a.m. until 11:30 a.m., and the abortion mill remained closed for the entire day. No women were exploited and no children were killed.

The police were caught totally off-guard by the rescuers and were unwilling to talk to any rescue representatives. As the police watched pastors Jesse Lee and Kirk Van Der Swaagh leading the rescue from near the abortuary door, they evidently thought they could disperse the rescuers by nabbing the leadership. (They didn't understand the dedication of rescuers.)

At eight o'clock, police climbed over the back fence of the abortuary, entered the back door, came through the building, opened the front door, climbed over the rescuers, and arrested the two pastors. They carried them over the rescuers' heads back into the abortuary, where the pastors prayed and preached to the officers until 10:30 a.m. Shortly after the pastors were arrested, two priests were also cuffed and dragged away.

Fathers John Vondras and Norman Weslin (who works for Mother Theresa's Missionaries of Charity) were squeezed through the front door to join Pastors Lee and Van Der Swaagh. As the police pushed to open the door wide enough to get them inside, the glass cracked on the door. The police officers then had the gall to charge both priests with criminal mischief! The police arrested and dragged everyone away. Bishop Vaughn was among those arrested, along with nine priests, two evangelical pastors, and one nun.

Everyone was charged with disorderly conduct except for the two pastors, who also got resisting arrest and criminal mischief. All rescuers were released on their own recognizance, and all believe the day was an exciting success.

Glory to God!

Pastors Only

In what is believed to be the first "pastors only" rescue to date, nine out of fifteen pastors were arrested at the West Ridge Ob-Gyn Group on May 18 when they entered the facility at 8:05 a.m. and refused to leave. The other six sat at the back door, but police refused to arrest them.

Three babies had been scheduled to die that day, and one was definitely saved as a result of the activity and the counseling given by the pastors.

The Rochester area was jolted as the media gave immense air time to the clergy rescue, covering it for several days. Media coverage extended beyond Rochester via USA Radio Network, AP, UPI, and CBN Radio.

May God raise up more courageous clergy in this desperate hour.

Atlanta: Waves of Rescues

At the onset, Operation Rescue drew 134 pro-life activists (most of them working people, fathers, mothers, students, clergymen, and retired people) to Atlanta for what was planned to be a one-week anti-abortion campaign from July 19-22, 1988. They planned to intervene in a nonviolent way to save women and babies in immediate danger of abortion.

A secondary purpose was to express opposition to the "abortion rights" plank in the Democratic Party platform.

As rescuers sang and prayed during "sit-ins" at the doors of the Atlanta SurgiCenter, the police arrived and arrested them. In order to identify with the nameless victims of abortion, the rescuers called themselves "Baby John and Baby Jane Doe."

The State of Georgia allows for the processing of defendants under an alias. By the end of the week, the City Solicitor's office agreed to process all the arrestees under their "Doe" names and release them for "time served." They had been in jail for four days.

At this point, an attorney representing the interests of the Atlanta abortion industry insisted that the Solicitor's offer be withdrawn, threatening to name the arrestees later in a civil suit. The City Solicitor capitulated to the attorney's demands and began insisting that arrestees give their names and pay a fine in order to resolve the case.

The arrestees rejected the new conditions. As a result, these brave pro-life rescuers were held week after week and threatened with fines and the possibility of a civil lawsuit. Hoping to revive the Solicitor's original offer, Operation Rescue called for wave after wave of rescuers to come to Atlanta.

During the first five weeks of rescues in Atlanta, nearly eight hundred pro-lifers participated in Operation Rescue. All have been arrested, and almost all have spent a few days in jail.

Atlanta: The Results

Operation Rescue is not merely a protest expressing a moral and political opinion. Rescues are designed to be effective, life-saving interventions.

During the rescues in Atlanta, children's lives were spared as their mothers turned from abortion and chose life.

Atlanta's supportive pro-life pregnancy services reported a sharp upsurge in clients coinciding with the Operation Rescue campaign. More women were calling and requesting information on alternatives to abortion.

Several of the female rescuers jailed in Atlanta were able to talk with an inmate who was pregnant and who had been scheduled for an abortion while she was in jail. Although she was under pressure from the prison authorities and her relatives to "get rid of it," she began to reconsider after reading some pro-life material. The rescuers put her in touch with a crisis pregnancy support service, and by the time she was released from jail this young woman had decided to carry the child to full term.

Other women rescuers shared the horrors of abortion with one of the female guards who was pregnant. Although this woman knew she was carrying twins, she was still contemplating abortion. After seeing pictures of mutilated aborted babies, however, she said, "If that's what is going to happen to my babies, then there's no way I can have an abortion." She chose life for her twins.

Because unselfish people were willing to go to jail for the sake of the children and mothers, they made an impact on the Atlanta prison population that will be felt for years to come. In addition to the children saved from death and the mothers delivered from exploitation, others received new life in Christ as a result of the Atlanta rescues.

Among those imprisoned for participating in rescues in Atlanta were nearly eighty pastors and clergymen. During their internment, prayer meetings and Bible studies were held daily, and the preaching was powerful! As a result of the ministry of these pastors and the faithful, loving witness of the other jailed rescuers, over thirty inmates received Christ as Savior.

The full results of the Atlanta rescues—in lives spared from the horrors of abortion or saved from the fires of hell—

may not be known in this life, but you can be sure the results are being recorded in heaven for all eternity.

Atlanta is not the end. Atlanta is only the beginning. As this book goes to press, more rescues are being planned in Atlanta and across the country.

Why Atlanta?

One pastor from the Atlanta area sent this letter to other pastors, encouraging them to participate in Operation Rescue.

Dear Friends,

I am a local pastor in the Atlanta area and have always taken a stand against abortion. I've preached against aborticide; prayed and fasted on special days in silent protest against the shedding of innocent blood; and participated, like many others, in supporting pro-life organizations.

On July 18, 1988, I was invited by a friend to attend a rally preparing people for the rescue to take place the next day in Atlanta. Within my mind a theological argument raged between nonviolent civil disobedience and obeying civil authority.

Two things convinced me to become involved:

1. My conscience in the Holy Spirit which gently nudged me to trust the Lord and walk by faith. (Romans 9:1)

2. The conviction that the higher authority of God's Law concerning the sanctity of life overrides the civil authority that has abandoned its responsibility and is protecting evil and punishing good. (Psalm 82:4 and Proverbs 24:11)

After being arrested in Atlanta for rescuing the unborn from death, I spent twenty-one days in prison. During this time God revolutionized my life. I found myself living the gospel of Jesus Christ. While incarcerated, I had the privilege of ministering to and counseling many people. I led twelve inmates to Christ and experienced God's Word in a new and living way.

Recently, a news reporter asked the question, "Why did Operation Rescue choose Atlanta to make a stand?" The answer is very simple: *Providence.*

I believe the Lord has raised up leadership out of obscurity and assembled people from many different denominations across the nation to unite them as a *witness* (a standard of righteousness) to testify to the church and to America that we need to repent for allowng twenty-five million babies to die since 1973.

God is challenging the church to raise up a standard of righteousness. It is time to take a stand. Watch and pray, asking God to speak to your heart concerning your place and participation.

Pastor Larry H. Baker
Word of Faith Church
Woodstock, Georgia

III
Abortion in America

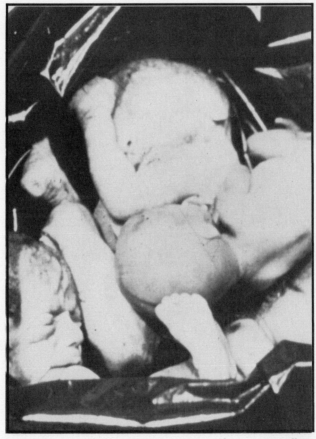

Hayes

Is it Really All that Bad?

III

Abortion in America

Is it Really All That Bad?

What's all the fuss about? you may be asking. *Is abortion really all that bad?*

Let's look at a few statistics that will reveal the scope of abortion in America.

- Every day 4,100 babies are reportedly aborted. (We don't know how many are killed but not reported.)
- Over one and a half million babies are killed by abortion every year.
- Between 1973 (the year abortion was nationally legalized via *Roe vs. Wade*) and 1983, the number of abortions increased 150 percent.
- In some cities, more women have abortions than give birth.

Who's having all these abortions?

- The typical abortion patient is young (62%), white (70%), unmarried (81%), and childless (56%).

- 60 percent of women having abortions did not make any attempt to use contraceptives at the time they became pregnant.
- 39 percent have had at least one previous abortion.
- 41-46 percent of teenage girls who got pregnant aborted their babies.
- Rape victims seldom get pregnant—only 0% to 2.2%.
- 98 percent of all abortions are done because the women "do not wish to be pregnant at this particular time."

(This statement was made by Dr. Irvin Cusher, UCLA Medical School, in testimony before a Senate subcommittee, 1981. He is a supporter of legal abortion.)

What about a woman's right to choose what to do with her own body?

Many people believe that abortion is just another surgical procedure that removes a piece of unwanted tissue from a woman's body. That puts abortion in the same category as appendectomies, tonsillectomies, and the extraction of wisdom teeth. But is that really what abortion is?

Abortion is expelling a human child from the protection and safety of its mother's womb. Sometimes this is done before the child is capable of sustaining life. Other times, the child would be old enough to survive outside the womb if he or she were not poisoned or burned to death. Hundreds of children survive abortion. Some live; most are denied medical attention and die.

Abortions fall into two categories: *naturally spontaneous* and *artificially induced.* Naturally spontaneous abortions are also known as *miscarriages.* The word *abortion* usually refers to the artificially induced procedure. Depending on the development of the unborn child, any one of six techniques may be used to induce abortions.

Suction Aspiration. In this procedure the cervix is dilated with a series of instruments to allow the insertion of a powerful suction tube into the uterus. The vacuum tears the unborn child and the placenta from the womb and deposits the dismembered child in a container. The arms, legs, head, and torso of the child are usually recognizable.

A nurse who assists with the procedure must reassemble the body parts to confirm that the uterus has been totally emptied. Leaving behind any tissue from the baby or placenta may result in bleeding and infection. Ninety percent of all induced abortions use this procedure.

Dilatation and Curettage or D & C. The cervix is dilated in the same way as for a suction abortion, but a loop-shaped steel knife is inserted to scrape the walls of the uterus. The baby and placenta are sliced to pieces and scraped through the cervix. Bleeding may be profuse. Failure to remove the entire contents of the womb may result in infection.

This method is most commonly used between the seventh and twelfth weeks of pregnancy and should not be confused with a therapeutic D and C done with a blunt curette for reasons other than undesired pregnancy.

Dilatation and Evacuation or D & E. A seaweed-based substance is inserted into the cervix to induce dilation. The opening must be larger because the developing child, usually twelve to twenty weeks old, has calcified bones and is much larger than the ones aborted in the two previous procedures. Forceps are inserted into the womb to dissect the child piece by piece. A special tool is used to crush and drain the head, which is usually too large to be removed whole.

Saline Injection. This procedure is used after four months when considerable amniotic fluid has accumulated around the unborn baby. A concentrated salt solution is injected through the mother's abdomen and into the baby's sac. The baby swallows this lethal solution and often reacts violently. For one or two hours he convulses and finally dies of salt poisoning, dehydration, and internal bleeding. Often his entire layer of outer skin is burned off.

The mother usually goes into labor within a day or two and delivers a dead, burned, and shriveled baby. Salt poisoning is the second most common abortion procedure.

Prostaglandins. Prostaglandins are hormones that induce labor. Chemicals developed by the Upjohn Pharmaceutical Company are injected into the amniotic fluid to induce the birth of a second-trimester infant who is still too young to survive outside the womb. The contractions are so violent that babies have been decapitated during the procedure. Some infants have survived their traumatic entry into the world, so salt or other toxins may be injected with the prostaglandins to prevent a live birth.

Hysterotomy. This procedure is usually used in the last three months of pregnancy, or in the event that saline injections or prostaglandins fail to produce a dead baby. Like a Caesarean Section, the womb is entered through surgery and the baby is lifted out. Without prompt medical treatment the infant will usually die, although some babies have been born alive.

Both prostaglandin and hysterotomy abortions have produced live births. Medical personnel, either by negligence or by a direct act such as suffocation or lethal injection have snuffed out their tiny lives. Failed abortions raise a lot of ethical questions and problems for the medical community.

Facing the Victims

Abortion must be exposed. Pro-abortion lies have so permeated and blinded our society through the liberal news media that many (or most) people are unaware of, or numb to, this holocaust.

One major cure for this numbness is pictures and films of abortion and its victims—the children. This forces people to come face to face with what abortion really is—a dead child. It is very hard to argue "a woman's right to choose" in the presence of a dead baby. It is impossible to call an abortion victim "a blob of tissue" when viewing the twisted arms and legs of an aborted child.

The news media usually won't print pictures or show film footage of aborted children because the images expose their pro-abortion lies. We must circumvent the media by distributing pictures of abortion victims and showing films like *A Matter of Choice* and *The Silent Scream.*

These films and others like them document that abortion is not a quick, easy operation, but a violent, degrading procedure that mutilates and *kills* a living, defenseless human being. (Information on how to obtain these films is provided at the end of this chapter.)

A Safe, Simple Procedure?

Do women really know what is about to happen to them during an abortion? Counselors at women's "health clinics" are known to have lied and deceived their clients into thinking abortion is a quick and safe procedure—and their only alternative.

Proverbs 12:6 states, "The words of the wicked lie in wait for blood, but the mouth of the upright rescues them." Pro-life counselors need to reach women with the facts, including risks and complications of the procedure.

Obviously, abortions are not as quick and easy as women are being told. Women face both immediate and long-term complications from the procedure.

Immediate complications include:

- excessive bleeding
- laceration of the cervix

•perforation of the uterus
•infection
•hepatitis from blood transfusions

Laceration of the cervix may occur in only 5 percent of first trimester abortions, but the *British Medical Journal* reported that nearly half of these women will lose their next *wanted* baby through miscarriage unless a physician reinforces their cervix with a special suture.

Lancet, a prestigious British medical journal, reported some sobering statistics. Out of 1182 suction abortions that these physicians performed, they reported 9.5 percent of their patients required blood transfusions and 27 percent developed infections. The doctors were dismayed that these complications were seldom mentioned by those who claim abortion is safe.

Long-term complications from abortion may plague women the rest of their lives. Perforation of the uterus and infection can do irreparable damage to the female reproductive system. When a hysterectomy becomes her only medical option, a woman is forever unable to bear children. Damage to the fallopian tubes, cervix, and uterine wall increase the risk of sterility, tubal pregnancies, miscarriage, and premature birth.

In addition to medical complications, many, if not most women, experience psychological problems, some traumatic. A women's immediate reaction to ending a problem pregnancy may be relief, but guilt, anguish, and depression frequently follow. Some women become suicidal or are haunted by flashbacks of their abortion experience. Others have recurring dreams about the child they'll never know.

Can a Woman Die From an Abortion?

A popular pro-life slogan states, "One out of every two people who enters an abortion clinic never comes out alive."

Abortion is designed to destroy the life of the unborn, but a woman who has an abortion also puts her own life at risk.

What have pro-abortion people said about the procedure? "Induced abortion is safer than childbirth; the serious complication rate for abortion is less than one percent; abortion is a good backup for contraceptive failures."

Reports investigating the number of deaths caused by abortions vary widely in their findings. Statistics range from 0.6 to 75 deaths per 100,000 abortions. Why the huge variation? Most deaths caused by abortions do not actually happen during the procedure, but afterward.

A woman may have an abortion on Saturday and think that all her problems are over. In reality, she may continue to bleed throughout the weekend. Severe loss of blood may result in shock. Infection frequently sets in when the unborn child is not completely removed from her womb.

Carrying a child nine months and going through the rigors of labor are safer than subjecting your body to an abortion. Because of our advances in pre-natal care, mortality from childbirth has decreased to nine deaths per 100,000 deliveries.

Telling the Truth

What have other medical personnel, who have nothing to gain from this multi-million dollar industry, discovered about this procedure?

> • "The impact of abortion on the body of a woman who chooses abortion is great and always negative. I can think of no beneficial effect of a social abortion on a body"—*Daniel J. Martin, M.D., Ltd. clinical instructor at St. Louis University Medical School, St. Louis, Missouri.*

• Pregnancy failure is increased 45 percent with one previous abortion—reported in a study published by *American Journal of Obstetrics and Gynecology.*

• A salt poisoning abortion has the highest fatality rate for the patient of any elective surgery, second only to cardiac transplantation.

• Neonatal deaths are 2-4 times higher in births following previous abortions.

• Approximately 98 percent of all induced abortions are performed for elective, non-medical reasons. Only 2 percent involve the life or health of the mother.

• Almost one in three pregnancies now end in an abortion, making it one of the nation's most commonly performed surgical procedures.

• A portion of the medical community once committed to saving lives has become involved in a $700 million a year abortion-on-demand industry.

Is Your Doctor a Murderer?

Dealing with the abortion industry may be difficult, but influencing your local doctor or hospital is much easier and more effective because your opinion is worth thousands of dollars. Most families can make an impact if they will make a *no abortion policy* their number one criteria in selecting the doctors and hospitals where they will spend their medical dollars.

Before you select a hospital for any service, first write the board of directors a letter. Call the hospital and request their names. Ask if they allow abortions to be done in their hospital. Request an answer in writing. Let them know that you are seeking a medical facility you can trust with all your health care needs.

Make an appointment with your obstetrician whether you are pregnant or not. No calls! Husbands, you go along. Explain to the doctor that you need to ask him some questions.

1. Does he do abortions? Yes or no. No explanations, please. You want an answer, not an excuse. Any medical person who can't give a straight answer to that question is probably performing abortions.

2. Is anyone else in their joint practice doing abortions? In some practices a certain doctor is the designated abortionist. That makes your doctor party to a crime.

3. Does the hospital he uses perform abortions or do they allow doctors to abort babies in their facility?

If there is any concern for any reason, as a steward of God's money you must inform them that your business will go to another doctor.

There is no room for compromise on this issue. The Scripture says: "Cursed is he who accepts a bribe to slay an innocent person" (Deuteronomy 27:25). These men and women are not doctors, they are executioners. Hands that murder innocent children should not have the privilege of delivering the children of Christians or anyone else for that matter.

Getting the Facts

The facts contained in this appendix were taken from pro-life material published by the organizations listed at the end of this appendix. If you would like to obtain copies of these materials, you can write or call their offices.

Americans Against Abortion
Box 70
Lindale, TX 75771
(214) 963-8678
Provide excellent pro-life materials from a Christian perspective. *Children...Things We Throw Away?* and *The Questions Most People Ask About Abortion* are powerful brochures.

American Portrait Films
1695 W. Crescent Avenue, Suite 500
Anaheim, CA 92801
(714) 535-2189
Producers and distributors of pro-life films such as *The Silent Scream; A Matter of Choice;* and *Conceived in Liberty.*

Hayes Publishing Co., Inc.
6304 Hamilton Avenue
Cincinnati, OH 45224
(513) 681-7559
Publish brochures, cassette and slide presentations, and other educational pro-life material.

Intercessors for America
P.O. Box D
Elyria, OH 44036
(216) 365-5184
Publishers of the booklets, *Abortion in America* and *When You Were Formed in Secret.*

National Right to Life Educational Trust Fund
419 7th Street, N.W., Suite 500
Washington, D.C. 20004
(202) 626-8809
Provide a variety of pro-life materials and brochures, including *Abortion: Some Medical Facts* and *The Challenge to be "Pro Life",* and *Abortion: What Do the Statistics Reveal?* They also publish a monthly newspaper.

Operation Rescue
P.O. Box 1180
Binghamton, NY 13902
(607) 723-4012
See *Information* section for a complete list of materials available from Operation Rescue.

IV

"I Had an Abortion"

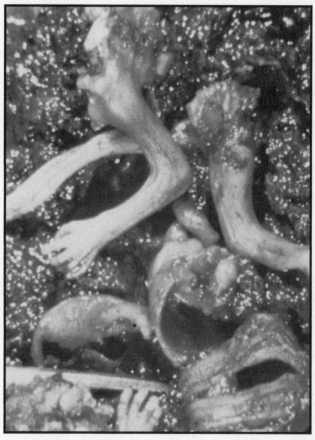

Hayes

One Woman's Story

IV

"I Had an Abortion"

One Woman's Story

Today there is an abundance of information circulating about abortion. Statistics and procedures are cold, hard facts. But what about the more subjective effects of abortion? How does abortion affect a woman on a personal level?

In this chapter, one young woman who had an abortion at the age of eighteen shares about her experience. While this is only one woman's story, the horror, the degradation, and the pain of her nightmare are typical.

We Were Getting Married Anyway

The decision to abort affects each woman differently. I can only speak for myself, but I know that everyone has a memory. I've known many girls who have had abortions, and all of them remember. Let me share my experience with you.

At the end of my senior year in high school, I had been dating the same guy off and on for four years. Our relationship was serious enough that everyone anticipated wedding bells, including us.

The act of sex that resulted in my pregnancy was pushed on my boyfriend's part and motivated by insecurity on my part. He was anxious for sexual intimacy, and I feared losing him. After having sex, I had a lot of regret but pushed my feelings aside. After all, we were getting married anyway.

That entire summer I didn't feel quite healthy. I told a friend that I hadn't felt right for months, but I never thought I could be pregnant. Finally, my mother took me to the doctor. He said there was nothing wrong with me—just that I was three months pregnant.

The doctor's news sent my mind reeling. Should I tell my parents? What would my boyfriend say? What about my plans for college? What about all my dreams? What should I do? Adoption? Abortion?

I felt ashamed—very ashamed. This only happened in movies or in books. How could it be happening to me? What would my boyfriend's parents think of me? What would other people think? I wasn't just scared—I was terrified.

I went out to the waiting room and asked my mom to come into the doctor's office with me. She knew before I even opened my mouth that something was seriously wrong because all the color had drained from my face. I felt horrible for the anger and hurt I was causing her. After leaving the doctor's office, we walked down the street together in silence as I desperately tried to hold back the tears.

Making the Decision

I dreaded my dad's reaction to the news. Instead of the raging explosion I expected, he was very quiet. With tears in his eyes, he silently went up to his bedroom. I had never seen my dad cry before. When he came back downstairs, he told me to call my boyfriend.

I told him the news as my parents listened. They insisted he come over immediately. Reluctantly, he came, and we talked privately. After a lengthy discussion about our options, the decision was made. I was going to get an abortion.

We both agreed that abortion was our best alternative because everything would return to normal. We'd never have to deal with it again. Aside from a few days of shock and havoc, our lives would be untouched and unchanged. Everyone would forget about it, and it would be over and done with. That's all I wanted.

Actually, I wanted to go back and make it different. I wanted to go back to when I wasn't pregnant, and stay that way! My parents weren't very happy with our choice because they were adoptive parents. But they told us it was our decision.

The next day I called the doctor to get the results of my blood and urine tests, which were positive. He needed an immediate decision because I was far enough along in my pregnancy that I would have to go through a more "advanced" procedure in a hospital if I waited.

The doctor referred me to Women's Health Services, and I scheduled an appointment. My mom and I went to the bank and got a money order to pay for the procedure. The clinic wouldn't take checks, only money orders. It was all set. There was nothing to do now but wait—and think.

As those three days progressed, I felt more and more alone. My boyfriend stayed away because he felt unwelcome in my parents' home, and indeed he was. I asked him to go to the clinic with me, but he refused. He told me he had to work, and he didn't want to sit in a waiting room with my mom. I was deeply hurt that he wasn't there when I needed him most.

The Nightmare Begins

Over the next three days, I wavered about what I should do. There was still time to change my mind. I could have the baby and put it up for adoption. Not being in any position to be a good mother, I certainly couldn't keep it.

If I carried the baby to term, I felt I couldn't just give it away. Being adopted, I had never known my mom, and I didn't want to have to adjust to never knowing my child. Yet, I questioned my right to end a life. Who was I to decide who should live and who shouldn't?

Those days were a horrible nightmare. I felt alone—very, very alone. Since my family felt it was my decision, they seemed to back away from me. But I wanted someone to walk in and tell me what to do. I wanted someone to tell me to have the baby and keep it and that they would take care of the finances. I wanted a miracle.

The night before I went to the clinic was the hardest. I spent most of the night up in tears. I didn't know if there was a God or not, but if there was, I needed Him then. Perhaps if I had heeded the convictions in my heart, I may have seen that He was right there with me. But I was blinded by my own evil intentions, and I didn't see Him. I questioned my decision, but in the back of my mind I knew I wasn't about to change it.

I never once thought of the life within me as a little baby. I knew once it was born it would be a baby, but for the time being it was just a blob that had created a major disturbance in my life. Somehow, thinking of it in that way made my decision easier.

I was uninformed about the stages of pregnancy and misinformed about what abortion really is.

The Worst Experience of My Life

After a night of tears and fitful sleep, the day finally came. My mom and I arrived at the clinic on time. My six-hour ordeal began in the waiting room where I filled out several forms. When my name was called, the worst experience of my life began. As I walked through the door that locked behind me, I felt more alone than I had ever felt in my life— and scared.

A pleasant receptionist went over the forms I had filled out, accepted my money order, and pointed me toward a bathroom where I was to give them a urine specimen. I left my sample on the shelf and followed the receptionist's directions to go to the lab.

While I was waiting for my blood work to be done, I was drawn into some small talk with the other clients. One woman said she and her husband didn't want another child. Another woman hadn't told her boyfriend because she didn't want to jeopardize their relationship. A repeat customer consoled the rest of us saying that ending a pregnancy was "nothing." The procedure would be over quickly, and it wasn't all that painful.

I anxiously glanced around the waiting room at the other clients. Some seemed nervous like me. But the ones who left the deepest impression were those who seemed so non-chalant. Their attitude put me more at ease, but it also made me wonder. I withdrew into myself to think.

After my blood work, I returned to the waiting room. That next hour seemed like an eternity. I wouldn't go any further until they had the results of my tests.

The battle in my mind raged on. There was still time to stop. Since I had come this far, I might as well go through with it, I reasoned. Just a few more hours and it will be over. Maybe the doctor was wrong, and they'd come out and tell me that I wasn't pregnant after all.

Abortion "Counseling"

My name was finally called, and I went in to see a "counselor." She told me that the results of my test were positive. I was *at least* twelve weeks pregnant, probably more. They wouldn't be sure until I was examined by the doctor—just before the procedure.

The clinic only compounded my confusion on what would be happening to me. Once the counselor explained the procedure to me, I *thought* I knew what I was doing, but later I discovered that she had omitted some major information.

The counselor told me that the procedure took approximately five to seven minutes. After receiving a shot in my cervix, the doctor would dilate it with a series of big instruments. I wouldn't need to feel apprehensive about the pain because of the anesthetic. The minor discomfort that I felt would be "just like monthly cramps."

After inserting some instruments, the doctor would determine the size of the fetus and the stage of my pregnancy. A vacuum machine would then "suck" the "fetus" out. The doctor would use another instrument to get any remaining parts. It was as simple as that.

The counselor *didn't* tell me that the remaining part would be the baby's head, and that the doctor would have to crush it to get it out. She didn't tell me that the vacuum machine would dismember, not a "fetus," but a little *baby*. She didn't tell me that recognizable arms and legs, not just blobs of tissue, would be ripped from my womb. She also didn't inform me that any movement during the procedure could cause the doctor's instruments to perforate my uterus. In fact, complications were never mentioned.

The counselor advised me to leave with some form of birth control so that I would not need a subsequent abortion. That sounded logical to me. After explaining all the forms of birth control, she asked me to make a choice. She encouraged me to take the pill because it was the most effective means. I consented. I would be given a two month supply when I left the clinic. That was the extent of my counseling.

The Damage was Done

I returned to the waiting room. The minutes dragged by. After what seemed like an eternity, my counselor approached. The time had come.

I was taken to a little "operating room" where I stripped from the waist down and donned a gown. When I came out of the dressing room, the doctor and his nurse were ready. I took my place on the table, placed my feet in the stirrups, and allowed the doctor to position me for his convenience.

First, the doctor examined me. The examination was not at all pleasant. He applied pressure to various parts of my abdomen, trying to feel the baby.

It had been hard for me to adjust to having strange men (and women) look and poke at my most private parts. This damaged my emotions in ways I didn't realize until much later.

After the examination, the doctor gave me the anesthetic, which was one of the most painful shots I have ever had. A sharp pinch was followed by intense heat. Next, I felt cramps, but they were the worst cramps I had ever experienced.

The doctor worked with a series of instruments for a couple of minutes trying to dilate my cervix. From what he told the nurse, I was more advanced in the pregnancy than they had first believed. The procedure continued and finally the vacuum machine was turned on.

Feeling my baby being torn from my womb was one of the worst sensations I've ever experienced. As the machine tried to suck out my insides, everything was trying to move up in my body to escape being pulled out. The vibration made me feel extremely nauseated.

I wasn't sure how much of this I could take. The counselor must have sensed my panic because she reassured me it was almost over. I grabbed her hand and squeezed it tightly until the machine went off.

The doctor instructed me not to move at all. My trembling body balked at such an order. The nurse was doing something by the machine while the doctor continued scraping my uterus. If this was a five-minute procedure, each second seemed to drag by.

Finally it was over. As I was lying there distracted by the counselor, the doctor left the room. I vaguely remember those first few minutes because of the tremendous pain and shock my body was experiencing.

Recovering From My Ordeal

I was given a pad to catch any bleeding, and after a few minutes the nurse told me I could get up and get dressed. When I sat up, I fell right back over. I had to lie there a long time before I could get up. The counselor had to help me dress because I was so physically drained. I felt as sick as I've ever felt in my whole life.

Once I was dressed, the counselor escorted me to the recovery room. Soft chairs lined the room, but all I wanted was a place to lie down. I had to get up every ten minutes, change my pad, and give the used one to the nurses so they could check my bleeding. It was embarrassing.

A few other women who had been through the same procedure looked fine. Only one or two women looked like I felt. A nurse informed me that my bleeding was normal. If I felt okay, I could go home. I told them I felt fine, so they let me leave.

Coming out of that clinic, I felt as if I had just lived through a nightmare. I felt humiliated, patronized, ashamed, cheap, degraded, and ruined—the whole spectrum of the most negative feelings a woman could ever experience. I felt so sick that I didn't even feel relieved.

Picking Up the Pieces

When we finally got home, I dragged myself up to my room and crawled into bed. My mom made me some soup while I tried to sleep away the pain. The stormy whirlwind of the past few days was over. Now I had to pick up the debris and go on with my life.

I dozed off for a while, and then my mom brought the soup up to me. Even though I felt nauseated, I was hungry. After eating, suddenly I felt normal again. Relief came flooding into my life. I was fine, and it was all over! Just like nothing had ever happened. No one would ever have to know—outside of my family and my boyfriend.

I wondered if my boyfriend had called to see if I was okay. Since this had been the most dangerous situation I had ever faced, I thought he should be concerned about me. He didn't call. I seethed with anger because I had suffered so much and he had gotten off "scott free."

I had gone through a personal hell that day, and he had gone through nothing. He didn't care about me. If he did, he would have been there when I needed him most. The promises he had made and all the caring words he had spoken were totally empty.

Less than a week later, I left for college. I wasn't aware that it *wasn't* all over. My abortion had permanently changed my life. I subconsciously filed the experience away in my mind to use against myself in the future. The emotional damage had been done; and unless I received healing, it would fester and infect my whole life. That's exactly what happened.

Conflicts and Complications

Once school began, I was relieved to be away from my boyfriend. I had become bitter toward him for influencing me to have the abortion. My trust in all men was shattered.

During my second semester in college, I developed a severe urinary tract infection that recurred at least a dozen times over the next two years. My doctor told me this was one of the many complications from abortions. Each bout with the infection reminded me of the pain and degradation I had experienced.

During my next year at college, I got seriously ill and discovered I had gonorrhea. When the doctor asked if I had ever had an abortion, he wasn't surprised to find out I had. He informed me that if certain sanitation codes weren't followed, a venereal disease could easily be transmitted with the instruments used during such a procedure. Because of the number of abortions performed in a clinic each day, it was more than likely that the instruments used on me had moments before been used on another patient.

In an effort to escape from the guilt and shame I felt, I went on a continuous binge of alcohol, drugs, and sex. My life was a shambles.

By the end of my fifth semester at college, I was flunking every class. I had become heavily involved in drugs and alcohol and was often suicidal. I hated myself and had no ambition or desire to live. When the college informed me not to return, I didn't even care.

Healing the Wounds

Although I was back at home with my parents, my problems did not go away. A deep, overwhelming loneliness continued to haunt me as my life went from bad to worse.

Then, I met a young woman who saw my despair and shared the love of Jesus with me. For the first time in my life I felt truly loved. I accepted Jesus Christ as my Savior and was water baptized.

Did my problems suddenly end? No. I knew God had forgiven me, but it took a long time before I was able to forgive myself for having murdered my baby.

A few years after I became a Christian, I married and experienced complications with the birth of my second child. My previous abortion had caused a weak spot in the uterus, and the placenta was not completely attached. Two months into the pregnancy I began to hemorrhage. Even after being hospitalized and released, I remained bedfast for ten weeks to prevent a miscarriage.

By the grace of God I wasn't sterilized by my abortion. Others have died from severe infection, shock, and loss of blood. Abortion is not a safe, simple procedure with low complication rates and minimal risks. It is a life-threatening, emotionally damaging, and degrading experience that no woman should ever have to go through.

Today I spend a lot of time counseling young women who are contemplating abortion or who are suffering from the after-effects. Only Jesus Christ can heal the deep, deep wounds that abortion causes.

I have also participated in a rescue at a clinic in the same city where I had my abortion many years before. Maybe my child would be alive today if, on the day of my appointment, I had found several hundred people blocking the entrance to the building. Sidewalk counselors could have provided the information I needed to make the right decision for me and my unborn child, and my life would have been much different.

Join with me in praying for young women who are looking for an alternative, and seek the Lord to know what you can do to stop this horrible mutilation and exploitation of an entire generation.

A Declaration

July Fourth In The Year Of Our Lord Nineteen Hundred Eighty-Eight

When in the course of a nation's history it becomes necessary for the God-fearing citizens of that nation to take actions which in times of peace would be considered drastic or extreme, a decent respect to the opinions of their countrymen requires that they should declare the causes that compel them to act.

We hold these truths to be self-evident: that God created mankind, and that all men and women, in-utero or out, are endowed by their Creator with certain inalienable rights, the first and foremost being the right to life. Governments are established among men to protect and defend the lives and God-given rights of its citizens. Governments and rulers that stray from their Divinely appointed purpose, and tolerate or participate in the oppression and slaughter of its innocent people, are held as barbaric and tyrannical, and history happily records the day of their downfall and just recompense. But before justice is restored to any such nation, before tyrants meet their end, courageous efforts from within or without must be made to break the bonds of tyranny. In such hours of crisis, it is the right and the duty of a nation's citizens to act in a manner which seems to them will best secure justice and safety for the oppressed, and for future generations.

We are in such an hour of crisis; an hour that is far darker and more grievous than the darkest hour endured by the original thirteen colonies under King George III;

an hour with more cruelty, murder, injustice, and exploitation than the founders would have dreamed possible. This is why our people must act. Let the facts, therefore, be candidly submitted to the world.

1967 marked the beginning of certain states legalizing child killing for reasons of convenience.

In 1973, a bloodbath was unleashed in all fifty states by the barbaric *Roe vs. Wade* decision. Seven despots, whose tender mercies are cruel, forsook their Constitutional responsibilities, and against all decency, common sense, scientific evidence, and natural and Divine Law, stripped our in-utero countrymen of their rights. They declared these children non-persons who could be slaughtered through the sixth month of gestation, for any reason, and until birth for the so-called "health" of the mothers. In the wake of this barbarism, doctors turned executioners have developed insidious means of destroying the defenseless. Let them be plainly told.

Children are suctioned out of the womb, limb from limb, until their twisted, dead bodies lie in a pile of human carnage.

Children are chemically burned to death by a salt solution injected into the uterus. This agonizing death takes from three to twenty-four hours, and has often resulted in live births.

Children are viewed on a ultrasound screen and hunted by the assassin's hypodermic needle containing drugs to cause heart failure. The needle is brutally, without anesthetic, plunged into the child's chest cavity and into the heart, causing heart failure and death to occur shortly thereafter.

Children are cut up and scraped out by curette.

Children too large for curette or suction are wrenched, twisted, broken, and torn piecemeal from the uterus by the murderers' forceps.

Children are expelled prematurely from the womb after the mother's labor is chemically induced. The violent contractions produced have literally decapitated children during labor.

Children too large to be aborted vaginally are aborted by C-section. This method, along with other techniques already mentioned, often results in a live birth. The child is then either injected with a deadly narcotic, smothered, strangled by the assassin, or simply left unattended in a bucket or wash basin to gasp for breath and slowly die. On a few such occasions, an attending nurse moved with pity, has actually saved the child in spite of orders to let the baby die.

In all, nearly five thousand children per day are butchered in ways that defy America to call herself a civilized nation.

The Supreme Court, in keeping with its cruel tyranny, ruled that pregnant mothers do not have the right to be told the possible physical and psychological side effects of abortion. Vulnerable women in crisis pregnancies are deceived, lied to, and exploited for the monetary gain of others. Women suffer laceration of the cervix, laceration of the uterus, perforation of the uterus, which is often accompanied by bowel perforation; infection, blood poisoning, and prolonged bleeding.

As a direct result of these injuries, tens of thousands of women miscarry in future pregnancies, thousands become sterile due to infection or scarring, and thousands more have had emergency hysterectomies, also leaving them barren for life. Hundreds of women have actually died under the "safe, legal" abortionist's knife.

Beyond that, millions suffer psychological and emotional trauma, deep depression, and nightmares; others turn to alcohol or drugs, and some, desperately wrestling with the guilt of a dead child, become suicidal.

Women have become the exploited second victim in this travesty.

Many courageous citizens have suffered harassment and arrest for attempting to prevent the murder of innocent children and exploitation of women; they have been prosecuted in mock trials; evidence for their defense has been suppressed; and many have been imprisoned for their defense of life.

The good citizens of this country have long sought redress to secure justice for children and mothers in conventional ways but have been rebuffed. All attempts at national legislation to stop the killing have failed. Pieces of state legislation seeking protection for children and mothers have been brought before the Supreme Court, whose incredible decisions have resulted in greater injury to children and mothers. The right of a father to protect his child has been abridged; the rights of parents to know if their minor daughter is obtaining an abortion have been denied; the right of the several states to demand that a truthful account of the child's development be given to the mother has been revoked; the right of the states to protect a viable child from murder during the seventh through ninth month of pregnancy has been overturned. Several states use taxpayers' money to pay for the murder of the innocent. The horrific truth is thus: The United States of America has endorsed the wholesale slaughter of more innocent people than virtually any nation in the history of the world. Over twenty-five million children are dead. A government that supports such heinous crimes, treating its weakest subjects with such cruelty, must be regarded as barbaric, tyrannical, and may soon be viewed by many as totally illegitimate.

At the very least in the meantime, the good citizens of this nation have no obligation whatsoever to obey or regard as legitimate any law that permits, supports, or protects the exploitation of women and the slaughter of innocent children. The people must move to protect the innocent and the exploited, since the government has abandoned its responsibility to do so.

Our once great nation, though always with faults, was born because of and founded on the concept of Higher Law; the belief that God, not man, was the Judge of the world, and that governments were accountable to Him, and that when they usurped His authority, they were no longer legitimate but tyrannical; the belief that it was the right and the duty of a people to challenge, alter, or abolish such tyrannical governments or despots that trod upon a people's God-given rights; and the belief that God would support and protect those who moved to challenge the authority of a government functioning against His will. With those beliefs, we heartily concur.

Therefore, we have committed ourselves to challenging and fundamentally altering the present status of American law, as it relates to in-utero children and pregnant mothers.

We hereby declare *Roe vs. Wade* and all subsequent court decisions and legislation which permit, support, or protect wanton child killing to be unjust, illegitimate, non-binding and unlawful.

We appeal to the Supreme Judge of the world, the God of these innocent children, the God who gave our country birth, to protect us, to vindicate our actions, and to restore justice to this wounded nation before it perishes. And with a firm reliance on Divine Providence, to the end of vanquishing this atrocity from our land, we pledge our Lives, our Fortunes, and our Sacred Honor.

(If you would like to obtain a copy of this declaration printed on parchment paper, contact Operation Rescue.)

About the Author

Randall Terry, a native of New York state and graduate of Elim Bible Institute, has been involved extensively in pro-life work for several years.

In May of 1984, Randy founded Project Life in Binghamton, New York. This educational and activist pro-life group operates The Crisis Pregnancy Center, where free medical services and support are offered to women who want to keep their child. In 1987, Project Life opened The House of Life, a home for unwed mothers.

Randy's study of the Scriptures and history led to his participation in rescue missions to save children from death and mothers from exploitation. For his efforts, Randy has been arrested numerous times in various cities and has spent more than sixty days in jail.

Since founding Operation Rescue in October 1986, Randy has led large pro-life sit-ins in several major cities, including Cherry Hill, New Jersey, New York City, Philadelphia, and Atlanta.

Information

For more information about Operation Rescue write to:

Operation Rescue
P.O. Box 1180
Binghamton, New York 13902
(607) 723-4012

If your organization would like to become an Operation Rescue affiliate, please contact:

Operation Rescue
Attn: Affiliate Information
P.O. Box 1180
Binghamton, New York 13902

Materials Available
from Operation Rescue

Literature

Pro-Life Newsbrief
A monthly publication providing information on upcoming rescues and reports on rescues in cities across the nation.

To Rescue the Children:
A Manual for Christ-Centered Pro-Life Activism
A comprehensive seventy page instruction manual on starting a Christ-centered pro-life ministry. Discusses sidewalk counseling, pickets, media, recruiting, and educating the public.

The Right and Responsibility to Rescue
A sixteen page booklet by Rev. Daniel J. Little answering objections about rescue missions.

Higher Laws
A tract outlining the scriptural examples of obedience to God's Law over man's law.

Psalter
A pocket compilation of Psalms, hymns, and prayers ideally suited for on-site rescuers.

Rescue Tract
Explains what rescues are and why they are a vital part of the pro-life movement. An excellent tract for pro-lifers to distribute in their churches, pro-life groups, mailings, etc., to recruit for and stage local rescues.

Audio Cassettes

When the Battle Raged
Includes four stirring songs, plus a motivating sermon on reaching out to pre-born children and their mothers.

Our Lives, Our Fortunes, Our Sacred Honor
Recorded inspirational messages by Randall Terry and by Bishop Vaughn, of the New York City Arch Diocese, on the eve of the New York City rescues.

A Call to Clergy
A challenging call to pastors from God's Word to be involved in rescues.

Rescue Training
"A Guide for Saving Lives" (four tape set). The complete audio transcripts of the rescue training videos.

Videos

Higher Laws
A deeply challenging call for Christians to rise up and peacefully grind the abortion holocaust to a stop.

Rescue Training
"A Guide for Saving Lives" (three volume set). Comprehensive videos that detail rescues in a ten-step outline to help pro-life leadership educate, train, and recruit for all aspects of rescues.

CBN—Operation Rescue
A brief, informative, and powerful overview of two actual rescues—Cherry Hill, New Jersey and New York City. Also includes a CBN interview with Randall Terry, Director of Operation Rescue.

Notes

Chapter 2

1. James and Marti Hefley, *By Their Blood* (Milford, MI: Mott Media, 1979), p. 202.
2. Robert Payne, *The Life and Death of Adolf Hitler* (New York: Praeger Publishers Inc., 1973), p. 218.

Chapter 4

1. *The Life of D. L. Moody* (Murfreesboro, TN: Sword of the Lord Publishers, 1979), p. 319.
2. Ibid., p. 333.
3. Amy Carmichael, *The Gold Cord* (Fort Washington, PA: Christian Literature Crusade), p. 22.
4. Ibid., p. 75.
5. Ibid., p. 37.
6. Arnold Dallimore, *Spurgeon* (Chicago, IL: Moody Press), p. 126.

Chapter 6

1. John Foxe, *Foxe's Book Of Martyrs* (Springdale, PA: Whitaker House, 1981), p. 12.
2. Ibid., pp. 21-23.
3. Corrie ten Boom with John and Elizabeth Sherrill, *The Hiding Place* (Old Tappan, NJ: Fleming H. Revell, 1971), p. 99.

Chapter 7

1. Carl Lawrence, *The Church In China* (Minneapolis, MN: Bethany House Publishers, 1985), p. 102.
2. Ibid., p. 114.
3. Hefley, *By Their Blood*, p. 256.
4. Ibid., p. 255.
5. Hans Kristian and Dave Hunt, *Secret Invasion* (Eugene, OR: Harvest House, 1987), p. 33.
6. Ibid., foreword.
7. *Christianity Today Magazine*, May 15, 1987, Chuck Colson, "The Fear of Doing Nothing," p. 72.
8. Dietrich Bonhoeffer, *The Cost of Discipleship* (New York, NY: Macmillan Publishers Co., Inc., 1963), pp. 242-243.

Chapter 11

1. Hefley, *By Their Blood,* p. 219.